RECONSTRUCTING INDIA

SIR M. VISVESVARAYA

K.C.I.E., M.INST.C.E.

GYAN

Published by

Gyan Publishing House
5, Ansari Road
Daryaganj, New Delhi-110002
Phone: 011-47034999, 9811692060
E-mail: books@gyanbooks.com

Distribution Network
gyanbooks.com
India, USA, Canada, UK, Australia, France

ISBN : 978-81-212-9434-8 (PB)
First Published, 1920

2nd Impression 2023

Printed at: Gyan Press, Delhi.

RECONSTRUCTING INDIA
Author: SIR M. VISVESVARAYA

RECONSTRUCTING INDIA

RECONSTRUCTING INDIA

BY

SIR M. VISVESVARAYA

K.C.I.E., M.Inst.C.E.

Lately Dewan of Mysore,
Formerly Superintending Engineer and Sanitary Engineer to Government, Bombay. Sometime Special Consulting Engineer, Hyderabad State

LONDON

P. S. KING & SON, LTD.

ORCHARD HOUSE, WESTMINSTER

1920

PREFACE

In view of the extensive changes which are now being made under the new Government of India Act, it is necessary to study Indian political, economic and social problems in a new light.

It is the spirit and intention of the Act to prepare the country for full responsible government, and it should certainly be the endeavour of the people to remove at once every stumbling block from their path and to take the most complete advantage of this new opportunity.

The Indian mind needs to be familiarized with the principles of modern progress, a universal impulse for inquiry and enterprise awakened, and earnest thinking and effort promoted. By these and other means a new type of Indian citizenship—purposeful, progressive, and self-respecting—should be created, and a self-reliant nationhood developed.

This book seeks to indicate, however imperfectly, the avenues towards reconstruction now open. It attempts, in a constructive spirit, to outline a scheme of true national life, and for the high task of achievement invites co-operation from all parties.

The author may claim some measure of administrative experience, as he has spent many years in the service of the British Government in India and in leading Indian States. He has, on several occasions, travelled outside India for the purpose of obtaining first-hand knowledge of world conditions and problems.

The book has had to be written whilst away from home and under other difficulties. The author is indebted to several friends and assistants for material help in its preparation.

M. VISVESVARAYA.

LONDON,
10th October, 1920.

CONTENTS

CHAPTER I

THE INDIAN PROBLEM

THE Great War subjected all countries to a severe test, revealed weaknesses in the political, social and industrial structure, previously unsuspected, and forced statesmen to undertake reconstruction on a comprehensive scale.

The first place in all programmes of reconstruction has necessarily been assigned to the repair of ravages wrought by war and the conversion of war machinery to productive use. Next has come the strengthening of national defence. Then have followed measures for increasing production, especially of manufactures and shipping, and the extension of foreign commerce, particularly the export of manufactured goods. Great emphasis has also been placed on the importance of extending education, and on the necessity of improving social conditions and raising the standard of living among the labouring classes.

India, happily, has had no devastated cities to reconstruct, no ruined homesteads to restore, and no sunken ships to replace. Her problem of demobilization has been comparatively small. She has, however, incurred for the first time a heavy unproductive debt, and has had to face the problem of high prices and food scarcity.

Reconstruction on an extensive scale is more urgently needed in India than in other countries, because political, social and economic developments have been insufficiently considered for many years past, and because, in consequence of such neglect, the standard of living has reached a level far below the minimum recognized in civilized communities as necessary for decent existence.

The Japanese Government fifty years ago undertook a comprehensive programme of reconstruction. The lead then given is still being vigorously followed. As a result, life in Japan to-day is one sustained effort toward self-improvement, and already the average standard of earning there is three to four times what it is in India.

As a dependency, India has had no reconstruction programme. She is, therefore, called upon now to begin much of the work which Japan has already successfully accomplished. She has to rebuild a structure dilapidated by the neglect of ordinary repairs.

One of the greatest deficiencies which India has to make up is her lack of facilities for securing education. To-day, three villages out of every four are without a school-house, and about 30,000,000 children of school-going age are growing up without any instruction. The officials have been so opposed to compulsory education that, until quite recently, they were disinclined even to permit municipalities willing to bear the cost to introduce such a system. No wonder that barely seven per cent. of the Indian population can read and write, whereas in progressive countries eighty to ninety per cent. of the population is literate.

The universities are utterly inadequate in number for so large and populous a country, and fall far short of modern requirements in equipment. The provision for technical and commercial education is meagre in the extreme.

Lack of liberality in this respect, and absence of official encouragement of indigenous enterprises, have kept Indians from developing new and expanding old industries and extending commerce. At the same time, the world competition has made it impossible for the indigenous industries to thrive. Indians have, therefore, been driven more and more to the land.

Nearly three-fourths of the population is solely dependent upon agriculture, which, owing to poverty and lack of education, is still conducted with crude, old-fashioned methods and implements, and without any scientific attempt to renew the fertility of the exhausted soil. The yield per acre is small, and the farmer is able barely to eke out a miserable existence. In spite of these chronic conditions, no provision has been made to enable the rural population to find profitable work by developing agricultural or cottage industries. This is especially to be deplored, because farming operations in India occupy only six or seven months out of the year.

The development of the natural resources of the country has been restricted because Indian directing energy has not been given free scope, and British direction available in India has been limited. Had Indians received support and encouragement from Government, they, with their old skill at handicrafts, might have produced manufactured goods at a rate that would have made them formidable competitors in the modern industrial world.

Substantial success in trade and commerce is impossible to-day without large capital and combines. In the United Kingdom, such combinations are encouraged and assisted by Government. In India, on the contrary, they are regarded as a menace to British trade and, therefore, to British supremacy, and discouraged.

Industry is even penalized. Excise duty is, for instance, imposed upon cotton manufactures. Canada taxes all imported goods; 15 per cent. on cotton goods from the

United Kingdom and 22 to 23 per cent. on those from the United States. The duty is put on with the express intention of protecting the Canadian manufacturer from foreign competition.

In India, on the other hand, not only are cotton goods imported practically free, but the government actually imposes an excise duty on the products of the local mills to enable the British manufactures to compete successfully with them. Nowhere else in the world would such an obvious attempt to handicap industry be tolerated.

Indians engaged in trade and commerce in foreign countries have no financial or political backing, and foreign intercourse is discouraged. Shipping, as an industry, has practically died out.

The cumulative effect of these policies upon the economic condition of the people has been most deplorable. An unskilled labourer in the United States or Canada earns more in a week than the Indian worker earns in a whole year. The estimated average wealth of the Indian population is less than one-twentieth of the corresponding average for the United Kingdom, and about one-thirtieth of that for the United States. And yet the 325,000,000 of Indians have not only to feed and clothe themselves, but also to support one of the costliest administrations in the world.

The low output of production in India is mainly due to the fact that men and women are engaged in a lower order of occupations there than in other lands. The higher occupations are under non-Indian control. While careers are open to Britons at home and abroad, wherever they may choose to carry on their life work, Indians find the doors of opportunity closed to them in their motherland, and are not welcomed even as labourers in civilized countries.

The present system of governance aims at preserving order rather than ensuring progress. Peace and security are maintained, moreover, by autocratic methods, and the activities of the people are restricted and their national growth stunted in the process. Again and again, during recent years, antiquated regulations have been employed to deprive Indians of liberty without charge or trial, and, not satisfied with these drastic powers, the administration, during the last decade, has armed itself with legislation enabling it to interfere with freedom of press, speech and movement in a manner unknown in any civilized country.

The people themselves are, as a rule, passive and unaggressive. They are guided rather by the opinion of the caste or community than by a common national standard of life, thought and work, by centuries-old traditions and superstitions rather than by the collective experience of the modern world. Foreign travel is interdicted. Through leaning on others, large numbers of people have become reduced to social parasites.

The existence in India of millions of persons of the depressed classes, whose very touch is considered pollution by the caste people, is to be condemned on humanitarian as well as economic grounds.

The backwardness of women's education, and the restriction of their employment to domestic duties and, among the agricultural classes, to casual field work, without their being given any recognized status or reward, is also holding back the country. It is inevitable that where such a large proportion of the population is kept unemployed or partially employed, or engaged in inferior poorly paid occupations, the *per capita* production should be very small, and the efficiency and prosperity of the nation, as a whole, very low.

The social customs of India promote a fairly rapid growth of population. Early marriage is the rule, and children are born into a world in which no provision has been made for their maintenance. In a country like Norway, where people marry at about 25, the rate of increase of population is slow, and it is, therefore, possible to maintain a high standard of living. India has still to learn that it is better to have a small, well-trained, prosperous population, than to have millions of half-starved, inefficient people retarding the progress of the country by their dead-weight.

Hope is to be derived, however, from the fact that India possesses potential energy of unparalleled magnitude. Her greatest asset is the inherent intelligence of the people. Though relatively to the total population the percentage of illiteracy is appallingly large, yet the aggregate volume of literacy compares very favourably with that to be found in European countries, not excepting the United Kingdom itself. As many, or more, children are attending educational institutions in India as in the United Kingdom. There are more under-graduates in the eight Indian universities than there are in all the universities of the United Kingdom.

Under favourable conditions, with stead-fast perseverance in a settled national policy, and by the introduction of science, modern machinery, and up-to-date business methods, the production of the country from agriculture and manufactures could easily be doubled within the next ten and trebled in fifteen years. Foreign trade could likewise be doubled in a similar period. In less than fifteen years the high percentage of illiteracy could be reduced to a fraction of what it is at present.

The constitutional reforms, sanctioned under the Government of India Act, of December, 1919, will, if worked in the spirit in which they were conceived by the British statesmen responsible for them, greatly increase India's opportunities. That such reforms were given so important a place in the British programme of reconstruction, demonstrates Britain's goodwill towards India. That a reasoned comprehensive scheme of this magnitude was matured, in spite of persistent opposition, and placed upon the Statute Book in times of great political unrest, is a tribute to the genius and earnestness of its sponsors. But for Mr. Montagu's perseverance and breadth of view, the reforms might have meant merely increased popular representation in the legislative councils, the people being left to fight the bureaucracy in order to obtain, one by one, the internal reforms they desired. The scheme has defects. Its scope might have been wider; but it is well-intentioned, and so far as it goes, complete.

It must be remembered that the people's standards are higher to-day than they have ever been in the history of Indo-British relations. In order to create conditions favourable to progress, there must be a radical change in the system of Imperial control over Indian affairs, and in the official attitude towards the people's aspirations and Indian problems generally.

The reforms scheme will doubtless give the people a substantial voice in local affairs, but that, in itself, will not be sufficient.

The public activities of the country have hitherto yielded scanty results, because they have not had a reasoned scheme of national life behind them. State policies, to be successful, must have for their sole aim the good of the people, and must be precise and adapted to their understanding, tastes and means.

There should, moreover, be an effective organization, independent of Government, to survey and catalogue the problems and needs of the nation, and to refer such problems to all classes of society for study, with a view to benefiting the country as a whole. This would create in the people the power of joint thought and joint action, and stimulate the growth of mass consciousness, the truest tests of a nation's efficiency.

It will be necessary to study world conditions as well as local conditions in order to discover the weak points in the Indian system. The deficiencies must, then, be catalogued and plans formulated. This book is an attempt, though a very imperfect one, in this direction.

Next, a favourable atmosphere must be created. It is hoped that the constitutional reforms will help to do this.

Thirdly, the leaders must carry on press and platform propaganda to stimulate the people. The masses must be made to understand India's position relative to modern conditions. They must be shown how the work that lies before the country is to be performed. Differences between the various communities or races, and between castes and creeds permanently residing in the country, must be sympathetically adjusted, and where possible, eliminated. The people must be taught to associate in their daily work for a common object and with common aspirations. They must realize that anything they may do to help each other will be a service to the motherland. Above all, the country as a whole must join in constructive effort with the rest of mankind.

If, as suggested in this book, the utilization of India's man power and material resources is placed in the forefront of national aims, if the people's general and technical knowledge is developed, if private initiative is stimulated, if all the latest inventions and discoveries are applied to increase production, if foreign experience is adapted to Indian conditions and fully utilized and useful foreign institutions readily adopted, if in short, all the improvements necessary and possible are introduced, the development of India, politically, economically and socially, will proceed at a pace which may be one of the outstanding features of the coming generation.

The immediate future will put all persons and institutions to a severe test. The forethought and vigour with which Indians apply themselves to their new task, their capacity for joint action, their ability to maintain harmonious relations between all races and communities, and the co-operation which they will be able to secure between themselves and Government agencies, will determine the pace of their progress.

If the British cordially help the Indians to build up their industry and trade, the resulting effect on India's prosperity will be immense, while the volume of benefit, even to Great Britain, will be far greater than it is at present. Such help will bind the two countries together by the strongest of links, namely, common interests.

British business interests and trade will assuredly not suffer in the long run. With increase of production, there will be gain all round—to the producer, to the manufacturer, to the middleman and merchant, to every one who takes part in building up the country's prosperity. With such growth, although British interests may, as time goes on, seem smaller relatively to Indian interests, there is no reason why they should not increase in actual volume, as has been the case in Canada. There is room for both Britain and India in the great reconstruction work that lies before the country. Both will benefit, if the exclusive or partisan spirit is replaced by sympathy and active co-operation.

CHAPTER II

INDIA IN RELATION TO PROGRESSIVE COUNTRIES

Before attempting to prepare a programme of reconstruction for India, it is necessary to consider her economic and social conditions, in relation to those of progressive nations, to discover where and why she lags behind. It will not be sufficient merely to compare her present achievement with her own past record. The results of such a survey may be hurtful to Indian pride, but if India aspires to occupy a dignified position in the comity of nations, she must face facts.

One has but to glance at vital statistics to realize the gravity of the situation. According to the census of 1911, the population of British India was 244,267,542, and of the Indian States 70,888,854; or a total of 315,156,396 for the whole Indian Empire. Accurate revised figures will not be available until after the census has been taken in 1921; but it is probably safe to estimate that the actual present population of India is 325,000,000.

In 1911 the population was spread over an area of 1,093,074 square miles of British territory and 709,583 square miles of Indian States, representing a total area of 1,802,657 square miles. Thus there was an average of 175 persons to the square mile for the whole of India. The density of population in British India proper was 223 and in the Indian States 100 persons to the square mile. The corresponding figures for the United Kingdom were 374, for Japan 356, and for the United States of America 31.

Although the average density of population is only 175 persons to the square mile for the whole country, there are districts in the Madras Presidency where the density goes up to 1,488. There are districts in Bengal with a maximum density of 1,163 persons and in Bihar and the

United Provinces of 882 persons to the square mile.

The United States, with a population of 91,972,266 persons, stands, among progressive countries, next to British India, with her population of 244,267,542. But while America has large resources of surplus arable land, in India all soil fit for profitable cultivation has long ago come under tillage. Usually the resources in such areas are taxed to the uttermost, and since at least three-fourths of the population are dependent on agriculture, even the partial failure of a single monsoon is often attended by widespread disaster. This is one explanation of the comparatively high death-rate and the low average duration of life in the country.

The average death-rate for all India for the past ten years has been 31·8 per thousand. The corresponding recorded death-rate in other countries is 21·9 in Japan, 15·12 in Canada, 14·6 in the United Kingdom, 14·0 in the United States of America and 10·5 in Australia.

The average life of an Indian is estimated

at 23 years, as compared with 45 to 55 in Western countries. Climatic influences are not to be disregarded, but in the main this is undoubtedly due to the low standard of living in India, and the lack of healthy and orderly growth of the population.

The average birth-rate in India for the past ten years has been 38·2 per thousand. The figure for Japan is 34·2, for the United States 31·3, for Canada 27·8, for Australia 27·7, and for the United Kingdom 21·1. Religio-social practices make for early marriage, and as a result the average birth-rate is so high that, in spite of the appalling death-rate, the population is increasing rapidly, approximately at a rate of five per thousand per annum. This may not prove an unmixed blessing, if new industries are not introduced and new careers provided in the country, or an outlet found for the surplus population outside India.

Of the 315 million people inhabiting India, including the Indian States, only 18,500,000 persons (16,900,000 men and 1,600,000 women) were returned as literate in the census of 1911. This means that only one out of every seventeen persons or 5·8 per cent. of the population are able to read and write. This was the state of affairs nine years ago. The percentage is perhaps slightly higher now, but it is deplorably low as compared with other advanced countries. The corresponding percentage of literacy is 95 in Japan, 94 in the United Kingdom, and 90 in the United States.

The number of existing schools for elementary education in British India is 142,203 and the number of pupils attending them is 5,818,730, of whom 5,188,411 are boys and 630,319 are girls. Taking all classes of educational institutions together, there is, in British India, one institution for every 1,717 persons of the population.

The school-going population in advanced countries varies from 15 to 20 per cent. or more of the entire population. Taking 15 per cent. only as a basis for calculation, the population of school age in India may be reckoned at 18,731,054 boys and

17,909,077 girls. The number actually attending the schools is 6,621,527 boys and 1,230,419 girls. That is, one boy out of every three and one girl out of every fifteen fit to be at school are actually attending educational institutions. The expenditure on education in British India from all sources, including fees, in 1916–17 was 11·2 crores of rupees,[1] giving a rate of Rs. 14·4 per head of school-going population or 7 annas per head of the entire population. The corresponding expenditure in other countries was Rs. 38 per head in the United Kingdom, Rs. 104 in Canada, Rs. 13 in Japan and Rs. 114 in the United States of America.

The provision for technical and commercial education in India is pitifully meagre. The students receiving technical and industrial education throughout all India numbered only 16,594 in 1917–18.

The statistics quoted show that the education of girls is neglected even more than that of boys, and that technical

[1] A note on the Indian currency and rates of exchange will be found on page 95.

education is practically non-existent. Most of the technical and commercial work of the indigenous population is being performed in an indifferent manner by persons who have learnt their trade by practice or who have obtained only home training of a rudimentary character. The Government and public effort in this direction has been negligible. It may be stated with truth that no serious attempt has been made to educate or to equip the nation for an industrial and commercial career, to enable it to earn a decent living and to hold its own amongst civilized nations.

The number of newspapers and periodicals published in India in 1917–18 was 3,978, which works out at about twelve per million of the population. The corresponding number per million persons in the United States was 225, in the United Kingdom 190, and in Japan 50.

There is a vast amount of Press activity in countries like the United States. It is recorded that the circulation of periodicals of all classes in that country, including dailies, reached, in 1914, the enormous figure of 205,000,000. Many of the dailies are made up of about 24 pages, imperial, the Sunday editions running to 100 pages or more.

The Press is a great educative force in all advanced countries, notably in America and the United Kingdom. In parts of the former country, the Press has taken upon itself the task of stopping corrupt practices and keeping the officials up to the mark in the proper discharge of their duties.

The indigenous Press of India is a poorly equipped and persecuted agency. We have Press Acts and Press control in varying degrees of rigidity both in British India and the Indian States, and the Press as a whole has no enthusiastic support in politically influential circles in any part of the country.

Except for a small expenditure annually incurred for purposes of coast defence, there is no Indian Navy to speak of. For decades, India has been entirely dependent for protection upon the British Navy: and this policy has not been revised even when other units of the Empire have been permitted to have their own navies. The depredations wrought, without any challenge, by the *Emden* in Madras, during the early period of the War, emphasized the necessity of creating an Indian navy.

In normal times, the Indian Army consists of about 70,000 British and 140,000 Indian troops, the latter officered entirely by Englishmen, making a total peace strength of about 210,000 of all arms.

Of the total British forces engaged in the recent Great War, the United Kingdom gave 75 per cent., all the overseas dominions together 12 per cent. and India 13 per cent.

During the War, the Government of India recruited, on a voluntary basis, over 600,000 combatants, and more than 400,000 non-combatants. Including the contribution made from the standing army India, therefore, in round figures sent on foreign service 1,300,000 men.

The annual military expenditure in India was £21,000,000 before the War, and has recently risen to the high figure of over £40,000,000.

The corresponding expenditure on defence in some of the other countries for 1913–14 is shown below :—

	Army. millions £.	Navy. millions £.
United States	30	27
United Kingdom	28	44
Japan	7·69	5·4
Australia	2·5	
Canada	1·5	

Although only a dependency and surrounded on three sides by the sea, and on the fourth by an almost impassable mountain wall, India spends on defence in normal times more than twice the amount required to maintain the Empire of Japan.

The number of post offices in India in 1917–18 was 19,410. Ten years previously (i.e. in 1907–8) there were 17,777 offices. Considering the vastness of the country, neither the present number nor the latest recorded decennial growth can be said to be adequate. The number of letters, newspapers, parcels, etc., conveyed by post offices in 1917–18 aggregated 1,147,922,768, giving a rate of 3·6 articles for every individual inhabitant. The corresponding rates in other countries were 147 in Australia, 123 in the United Kingdom, 136 in the United States and 34 in Japan.

The number of telegraphic messages conveyed in India during 1917–18 was 19,897,787 or 6·3 for every 100 inhabitants. The corresponding rate in the United Kingdom was 198, in Canada 154, and in Japan 73.

The telephone has come very largely into daily use for business in all advanced countries. According to the latest statistics available, the number of telephone instruments in use for every 10,000 inhabitants was 1,850 in Chicago, 1,170 in New York, 800 in Montreal, 480 in Sydney, 390 in London, 200 in Tokyo, and only 4 in Bombay and 3 in Calcutta.

Production may be considered under two heads, namely, agriculture and industries, the latter including mining, fisheries, etc. Under agriculture, British India has a cultivated area (including double cropped land) of 265,000,000 acres, of which nearly 47,000,000 acres are irrigated.

Taking good and bad years together, the value per acre of irrigated crops, in normal times, may be put down at Rs. 50 per acre and of dry crops at Rs. 15 per acre. The total agricultural production before the War was valued at about Rs. 562 crores or £375,000,000. The estimates of production under agriculture for other advanced countries are: The United States, £4,277,000,000; Japan, £300,000,000; Canada, £247,000,000; the United Kingdom, £239,000,000, and Australia, £73,000,000.

The statistical information available regarding Indian industries is very inadequate, although accurate information in this respect is especially necessary in the case of a country so industrially backward as India. Basing the estimate upon a knowledge of what is going on in the Provinces, the production from industries may be reckoned at about one-fifth of that from agriculture.

The total production of British India, excluding the value of live-stock, minerals, fisheries, etc., may roughly be estimated at £450,000,000, and the total, including all these sources, will probably not exceed £600,000,000. This gives a rate of production valued at about Rs. 36 per head of the population.

These figures are in the nature of a guess and presumably tentative. In view of the poverty of the people, it is important that a more correct balance-sheet of their resources be maintained, so that both the Government and the people may keep the figures in mind and endeavour to improve conditions from year to year.

The *per capita* production in the United States and Canada is £40·6 and £29·5 respectively under agriculture and £46·0 and £72·1 under industries. There is no reason why corresponding figures should not be available for India, but, as a matter of fact, they are not.

In India, the production under factory industries is very small compared with that under agriculture, and insignificant in comparison with other leading manufacturing countries.

The value of imports, both merchandise and treasure, into British India amounted to £109,570,000, and of exports from the country to £163,263,000 during 1917–18. The total sea-borne trade was £272,833,000.

This gives a rate of £1·1 per head of population, without making allowance for the population of the Indian States. If that allowance be made, the rate works out to £0·9 per head. The corresponding figures for other countries are: £62·6 in Canada, £40·0 in the United Kingdom, £37·2 in Australia, £17·0 in the United States, and £6·4 in Japan.

India exports raw materials and food products, while she imports chiefly manufactured goods. She has lost the power of producing the manufactures required for her own use, and is obliged to pay for her imports by growing more raw products. If she were to manufacture for her own wants, using her abundant raw materials and the millions of people at present insufficiently employed, she could not only produce all she required, but also export manufactured goods for profit. By so doing she could save much of the money she now pays for her imports, and could amass additional wealth by exporting manufactured goods. By reducing the pressure on the land the *per capita* production in agriculture will also be increased.

India has, for every million of her population, 115 miles of railway. The corresponding figures for other countries are: Australia, 4,955; Canada, 4,825; the United States, 2,533, and the United Kingdom, 515.

The tonnage entered into and cleared from British Indian ports in 1908, 1913 and 1918 was 12·9, 17·3 and 10·9 million respectively.

The old shipping industry has gradually died out, and the construction of new shipping is not encouraged. There are practically no large ships owned by Indians, and the coastal shipping registered at the Indian ports during 1917–18 was only 16,872 tons. On the other hand, the Government of Canada has been encouraging national shipping and foreign trade, with the result that her people now own roughly 1,000,000 tons of shipping, and her foreign trade has overtaken and exceeded that of India.

In the United Kingdom, the United States, Canada and Japan, special attention is at present devoted to the construction of shipping as an urgent after-war measure. No such move is visible in India, nor, under present political conditions and policy, does it seem possible.

The total gross revenue of British India, including the Provinces, in 1917–18 amounted to £109,000,000. The net revenue amounted to a little over £80,000,000. Of this, the revenue from land was £21,000,000. This net revenue gives a rate of £0·34 for British India, per head of population. The corresponding figures for other countries are: The United Kingdom, £19·3 ; the United States, £7·9 ; Australia, £7·5 ; Canada, £6·45, and Japan, £1·5. These figures for revenue do not represent the same type of taxation in all these countries, and the comparison, therefore, gives only a rough indication of the real state of affairs.

Three presidency and eighty-eight joint-stock banks have their head offices in India. In addition to these, ten exchange banks do business in India, but have their head-quarters outside that country.

There were 359 banks and branch banks in India in 1917. The corresponding figures for other countries were: The United States, 28,913; the United Kingdom (1918) 9,357; Japan (1916), 5,874, and Canada, 3,327.

The capital of indigenous Indian banks was £5,000,000. The British and foreign exchange banks had a capital of £18,000,000, making a total of £23,000,000. The corresponding figures (in million £) for the United States were 482; the United Kingdom, 88; Japan, 67; and Canada, 23.

The deposits (in million £) in Indian banks amounted to 118, those in the United States of America to 5,767, in the United Kingdom to 2,355, in Japan to 494, and in Canada to 324.

The position of India in the banking world "illustrates how trade follows the bank as much as the flag. The comparatively few branch banks and small deposits are striking in the case of India."[1]

At a rough estimate, the entire assets of India, including the value of land, buildings, furniture, gold, silver, live-stock, factories and other property, amounted to £3,500,000,000 before the War. This, distributed among the population of British India, works out to about £14 per head. The corresponding figures for other countries were: The United States, £391; the United Kingdom, £320; Australia, £262; Canada, £259; and Japan, £52.

The estimated annual income of British-India was, as already stated, £600,000,000, and the average income of an Indian was Rs. 36. On account of the high world-prices it may, perhaps, at the present time have risen to Rs. 45.

The Postal Savings Bank deposits in India amounted to Rs. 1,659 lakhs (£110·6 million) in 1916–17. This works out at Rs. 0·6 or annas 10·7 per head of population. The corresponding figures for other countries are: The United Kingdom, Rs.

[1] *Indian Finance and Banking*, by G. Findlay Shirras.

77·3; Canada, Rs. 14·85; the United States, Rs. 3·78, and Japan, Rs. 8·4.

Both here and in subsequent chapters special reference is made to conditions in Canada and Japan; Canada because that Dominion will in the nature of things be India's future model, and Japan because it is an Asiatic country which has adopted European civilization.

The figures given in this chapter have been taken from the most reliable sources available, but they do not in all cases represent the same group of conditions or transactions, and in a few instances they do not even pertain to the same year. The information could not be made more specific without elaborate explanations and qualifications, but it is hoped that, even so, they do indicate a rough comparison of existing conditions in India, relative to the countries quoted.

Political and Administrative Reconstruction

CHAPTER III

THE CENTRAL GOVERNMENT

THE Government of India Act, passed in December, 1919, leaves no portion of the administrative structure unaltered, though the changes made in some parts are much greater than in others.

In the sphere of local government, for instance, the principle of governance has been radically altered. Local bodies are no longer to be kept in leading strings, but are to be self-governing.

The Provincial Government has been divided into two parts; one part is to remain outside legislative control, while the other is to be placed upon a constitutional basis.

While the Central Government is to remain uncontrolled by the legislature, and is not to be federalized, it will have to submit to greater criticism from popular representatives. In matters in which it may be in agreement with its legislature, it is, as a rule, to be free from intervention by the Secretary of State. The provincial authorities will also be generally free from intervention from above in matters in which the executive and legislative organs are in agreement.

The position of the Secretary of State is to be altered by the establishment of similar conventions. He is further to be relieved of responsibility for purchasing stores and in allied matters, such responsibility being transferred to a High Commissioner appointed by and responsible to the Government of India.

The writer proposes, in this chapter, to examine in detail the changes effected in the administration of national affairs, and in the next three chapters to deal with those pertaining to provincial and local government and finance.

The decision of the Joint Select Committee that "India is not yet ripe for a true federal system," is to be deplored for two reasons, namely :—

(1) Not until the Government of India has been federalized on the Canadian or Australian basis, that is to say, not until the functions of the Central Government are limited to the administration of national affairs and its intervention in provincial affairs reduced to the lowest possible minimum, can there be anything like full provincial autonomy.

(2) As realized by the authors of the Joint Report "a federal system would have made it easier for the Indian States, while retaining the autonomy which they cherish in material matters, to enter into closer association with the Central Government."

The Act does not provide at all for the representation of Indian States in the Indian Legislature. That is an important omission, for those States will continue to lack, as hitherto, the opportunity of influencing the course of action in regard to (1) the disposal of public funds to which they indirectly contribute and which are appreciable, and (2) the administration of affairs which concern them jointly with British India.

"The Princes' Chamber" is designed merely to deal with large questions affecting the States. At best, such a council is an anachronism. The system of representation provided for shows that the British Government assumes that the Rulers represent the interests of their States. Many among them, no doubt, seek to promote the well-being of their subjects, but however progressive they may be individually, not all of them can be expected to surrender their autocratic powers or to discuss and deal with interests, policy and measures on terms of equality with the expert officials of the Government of India.

The Indian States will have to adopt constitutional government on the model of the reconstituted provincial administration if they are not to lag behind British India. For economic and social betterment, it is imperative that the people should be given the power to think and act in their own interests, the rulers gradually assuming the rôle of constitutional Sovereigns. The larger among the States will eventually need two chambers—a popular legislative council and a senate, in the latter of which due weight will, no doubt, be given to birth, property, education and experience.

Internal reform cannot, however, suffice. The affairs of Indian States are inextricably mingled with those of British India. Only by the creation of a federal system in which the Indian States are given a voice adequate to protect their interests and they, as well as the provinces, possess full autonomy, can the Indian problem be satisfactorily solved.

The three great self-governing Dominions have federal constitutions. The introduction of responsible government in India will not be complete until the Indian provinces are independent of the Central Government in local affairs, as is the case in Canada. Since the Dominion or the federal system of government is the accepted model, although it is to be reached by stages, the Government of India will be expected to place that ideal before the various departments of the administration and the public, and to make preparations to that end according to a regular programme.

The Government of India, as reconstituted, will consist of the Governor-General and an Executive Council. The number of members to constitute the Council is not statutorily limited. Three members of that Council will continue to be public servants or ex-public servants who have had not less than ten years' experience in the service of the Crown in India. The law member will have definite legal qualifications, but in future he may have gained those qualifications in India, and not, as hitherto, necessarily in the United Kingdom.

Not less than three members of the Council will be Indians. The Joint Select Committee took care to point out "that the members of the Council drawn from the ranks of the public servants will, as time goes on, be more and more likely to be of Indian rather than of European extraction."

It is to be hoped that these recommendations will be carried out in a liberal spirit. Rapid Indianization of the personnel of the Central Government is necessary to ensure the administration of affairs in consonance with Indian ideals and wishes. That, moreover, is the only manner in which Indians will ever become fit for self-government. It hardly needs to be added that only competent men should be appointed. If sufficient trouble is taken to select for each post the right man, and one acceptable to the Legislative Assembly, it will be found that there is no lack of good material in the country.

It is further to be hoped that the removal of the statutory limit will be utilized to increase the number of members of the executive councils. Canada, though containing a population only a fraction of that of India, and enjoying a smaller revenue, has more than twice as many ministers as India is to have, without reckoning the special ministries created during the War.

The Government of India, as thus reconstituted, will deal with matters affecting the defence of India—army, navy and air force; railways, shipping, posts, telephones and telegraphs; customs (including cotton excise); income-tax, banking, insurance, public debt; civil and criminal law; science, inventions, national and foreign trade and commerce. It seems a pity that civil law and the control of industry have not been left entirely in the hands of the provincial administrations.

The Indian Legislature as reconstituted will be bicameral, consisting of :—

(1) A Legislative Assembly comprising 144 representatives, of whom 103 are to be elected and 41 nominated, including 26 official members; and

(2) A Council of State, something in the nature of a senate, with 60 members, of whom 33 are to be elected and 27 nominated, including not more than 20 official members.

Since communal electorates have been constituted, it is to be feared that in some cases persons of proved political sagacity and trained in dealing with public questions may not find admission, and that important interests may be ignored. The present arrangement has to continue for some time, but, as suggested by the Joint Committee, it is to be hoped that the principle of proportional representation will eventually be adopted.

The electorate for the Legislative Assembly comprises 687,100 votes for general seats, 206,640 for Moslem seats, and 15,000 for Sikhs, a total of 908,740 votes.

The electorate for the Council of State is on a more restricted franchise, and the constituencies will only include 2,000 to 3,000 voters each. The total electorate for the Council of State may, therefore, be 70,000 to 80,000 voters.

The Presidents, at first appointed by the Crown, will, after four years, be elected by the Chambers themselves.

The Legislature is not to be a sovereign body. The members may criticize, but cannot control. The watch-dogs may bark, but they cannot bite. The executive is to be permitted to retain its autocratic powers until Parliament considers that the Legislative Assembly can be vested with further authority, which should be, at the outside, ten years from now.

The Indian Budget will be submitted to the Legislature, which will be free to vote upon it, excepting certain reserved charges, such as interest and sinking-fund on loans, salaries and pensions and national defence.

The Governor-General-in-Council has power to sanction any expenditure that may be refused by the Legislature, if, in his opinion, it be necessary or urgent. The Act, however, provides that every such case shall be submitted to Parliament, and that, before being presented for the Royal assent, it shall lie before both Houses of Parliament for at least eight full days of session.

If the administration is to work smoothly, the Governor-General should be guided by the wishes of the people's representatives, as in the self-governing Dominions. The Governor-General of Canada, for instance, has the power to veto legislation, but he never uses it. The Ministry is responsible for every Act, the Governor-General's power and authority being similar to that of the King in the United Kingdom. The Dominion Parliament cannot be dissolved without taking the advice of the Ministry.

All discussions in the Legislature should be open, ensuring correct and speedy decisions, and providing a species of political education for the people. In other respects, too, it is to be hoped that the new Legislature may prove as modern and progressive as those existing in the self-governing Dominions.

No provision is made for payment of salaries to members. In India, with its great distances, it is absolutely necessary that members should receive a salary, as in the United Kingdom, Canada, and other constitutionally governed countries. It is hoped that the Indian Legislature will itself take steps to bring about this reform.

The Legislature will be called upon to deal with a variety of highly complex, urgent problems. India is not only large and populous, but her standard of economic development is low, and she is extremely poor. At every step, foreign and Indian interests clash. The refusal to constitute a federal system of Government will keep the Government of India highly centralized.

It is imperative, therefore, that at least the popular chamber should have a long annual session to permit the adequate discussion of vital questions, and also to ensure that the executive, which has not been made responsible, administers affairs in consonance with popular wishes. No statutory limit has been imposed, and rightly, because each House of the Legislature should be free to settle such matters for itself. If the Legislature is left unfettered, it will, no doubt, follow the example of the Imperial Parliament, and sit for not less than 200 days a year.

To ensure that the administration of the various departments of State will be carried on according to Indian wishes, and also to provide opportunities for administrative training to Indians, standing committees of the Legislative Assembly should be formed at the beginning of each session. These committees may be attached to any department of government, and would serve the double purpose of keeping the official element in touch with public opinion and of securing attention to all important problems in which the public is interested.

Commissions composed of members of the Legislature, experts, officials and co-opted members should be constantly at work investigating conditions and making recommendations on the more important and delicate problems, including those affecting Imperial and international interests. The officials may join in the deliberations and advise, but need not vote. A Commission should be allowed to appoint its staff during the period of its existence, and should be free to correspond with foreign Governments for the purpose of collecting information.

In Japan, committees on which officials and non-officials co-operate exist for purposes of promoting education, agriculture, industry and the like. India may advantageously follow that example.

To investigate questions connected with the Central Government, particularly in its relation to the Home Government and the Provinces, the Central Government should send deputations to and maintain agencies in the self-governing Dominions and also in Japan. These agencies will study questions connected with preparation for autonomy, and supply any information required by the Central and Provincial Governments.

If the central administration is to be rapidly raised to the position of an autonomous Federal Government, it will be necessary to standardize plans of action. As policies, practices or Acts are completed, they should be immediately codified and put into operation as accepted facts. This process of standardization will be a guarantee of the steady progress for the necessary development work and the preparation for autonomous government.

Apart from providing such machinery, the urgent work of development will require at least three new ministries, viz.: (1) a Ministry of Reconstruction, (2) a Ministry of Conservation, and (3) a Ministry of Labour and Civics.

The Ministry of Reconstruction would deal with the many urgent problems mentioned in this book, bound to arise in the transition from dependency to autonomy.

A Ministry of Conservation will be needed, if only to co-ordinate the efforts of departments and agencies concerned with material development.

A Ministry of Labour and Civics will be required to train the people for new occupations and for the opportunities afforded by the new powers of local government—a branch of education woefully neglected in the past.

The new Act provides that, at the end of ten years, stock shall be taken of the work done, and recommendations made as to further administrative developments. The Indian Government should lose no time in formulating its ideas as to the various changes that may be needed, and taking practical action to bring them about.

The Government of India must abandon

its policy of contenting itself with the day's work and neglecting preparations for the future. Its success in the new era will be measured by what it will be able to accomplish in the next decade, to fit Indians for Dominion autonomy.

It has already been noted that the Government of India is to maintain its own High Commissioner in London, to discharge "agency" duties which hitherto have been attended to by the India Office. That High Commissioner will have functions and powers analogous to those of the High Commissioners of the Dominions. India should be also granted the privilege, enjoyed by the Colonies, of sending her own representatives and High Commissioners to the principal countries of the world, for trade purposes. The Dominion of Canada, for instance, has recently been allowed to maintain a diplomatic representative of her own at Washington—a new departure even for a self-governing Dominion.

With the creation of an Indian High Commissionership in London, the India

Office will, in future, deal solely with political matters. This change has been signalized by an innovation, which makes the salary of the Secretary of State a charge upon the Imperial treasury instead of that of India.

Under the new scheme, the control of the Secretary of State over Indian fiscal matters is being relaxed. The Joint Select Committee prescribed that India "should have the same liberty to consider her fiscal interests as Great Britain, Australia, New Zealand, Canada and South Africa," and "the Secretary of State should, as far as possible, avoid interference with the Indian fiscal policy when the Government of India and its Legislature are in agreement." His "intervention, when it does take place, should be limited to safeguarding the international obligations of the Empire or any fiscal arrangements within the Empire to which His Majesty's Government is a party."

A standing committee on Indian affairs of both Houses of Parliament is to be appointed, at the beginning of each session, to advise the Secretary of State during the difficult period of transition that lies ahead.

Sooner or later, it is presumed, there will be a constituent Assembly or Council for the British Empire. India should claim, on such a body, the position to which her size, importance and services to the Empire entitle her.

India was permitted to send her representatives to the Peace Conference; but no Indian representative was invited to the subsequent conference at Spa, although the representatives of the Dominions were so invited. The new Indian Legislature must see to it that she is not ignored in future conferences. All representatives of India in foreign countries should, moreover, be Indians.

Having been admitted as an original member into the League of Nations on terms of equality with the Dominions, she must see to it that the mode of representation is such as to ensure the accurate expression of Indian views.

CHAPTER IV

PROVINCIAL ADMINISTRATION

THE Government as reconstituted in each of the eight major provinces [1] is to be of a dual character. The part controlling the "reserved" subjects—namely, police, justice, land revenue, forests (except in Bombay) and water supply, including drainage and irrigation—is to consist of the Governor and the Executive Council, half Indian and half British, and is to be independent of the Legislature. The "transferred" subjects—namely, local self-government, and the departments of education, local industries, industrial research, public works, agriculture, forests (in Bombay), medicine and excise—are to be

[1] Madras, Bombay, Bengal, the United Provinces of Agra and Oudh, the Punjab, Bihar and Orissa, the Central Provinces, Assam.

administered by the Governor and the Ministers, generally with the consent of the Legislature.

The great majority of members of the Legislative Council will be popular representatives elected partly on a territorial and partly on a communal basis. In Bombay, for example, eighty-six of the 111 members will be elected. The number of voters in that presidency will be about 776,000. Each elected member, therefore, will represent on an average about 9,000 voters. The total electorate for all the Provincial Councils in the country will number about 5,200,000.

The Joint Select Committee clearly laid down that Ministers must enjoy the confidence of the elected majority; that they shall be given the fullest scope in their own sphere, that Governors shall accept their advice and promote their policy wherever possible; and also that members of the Executive Council shall afford all possible help and sympathy in dealing with proposals for development in the various departments. While anticipating that much advantage would result from such co-operation, they insisted that the duties of the two parts of the Government should not be permitted to become confused nor their separate responsibility obscured.

The provincial revenues and balances are to be allocated between the two sides of the Government under rules so framed as to make friction unlikely. If, however, the Members of the Executive Council and the Ministers cannot agree as to their respective shares, the Governor may make such allocation as he may think fit, and, if necessary, can refer the question to such authority as the Governor-General may appoint. Pending the adjustment of claims, the total provisions under different heads of expenditure in the provincial budget for the preceding year are to hold good.

Difficulties are certain to arise at the outset. Unless the Ministers selected from the Legislative Council are business men or otherwise trained in the conduct of affairs, they will need a little time to master the executive work of administration. The heads of departments, the majority of whom will be British officials, may not, it is feared, prove entirely sympathetic. On both sides tact will be required, and the patience and capacity for compromise of all concerned will be put to the severest test.

It will not merely be a question of every one attempting to do the right thing. The Government of India Act assumes that the electorates will be inexperienced in carrying on responsible government, and the Ministers in conducting executive work. Behind all, in the background, however, will be the influence of vested interests, of which the Act takes no account whatever.

The only manner in which difficulties can be overcome, conflict avoided and popular interest secured is for the entire Government to perform their functions in a constitutional spirit. A former Under-Secretary of State for India went so far as to state in the House of Lords, in the course of the debate on the Government of

India Bill, that the "reserved" subjects "will have to be controlled with a very strong constitutional strain influencing them." Since the people's chosen representatives are to predominate in the legislative councils, only such policies as find legislative support should be put into effect. As the interests of the people become the interests of the Government, friction will be lessened, harmony promoted, and progress ensured.

Considering the subjects to be dealt with, more Ministers will be required than the four apparently contemplated. Canada, with a population of only 8,000,000 persons, has eighteen Ministers. Some of the Indian provinces have a population exceeding 40,000,000 persons, so there is nothing unreasonable in asking for at least twelve Executive Councillors and Ministers for the larger provinces.

As suggested by the Joint Select Committee, the salaries of Ministers should be voted by the respective Legislative Councils. The salaries of members of the Council, which at present range from Rs. 56,000 to

Rs. 64,000, are excessive. Ministers should not be paid more than Rs. 36,000 per annum, though they may be given suitable travelling and entertainment allowances. In Canada, Ministers receive only about Rs. 21,000, while in Japan they receive but Rs. 14,400.

There might be two grades of Ministers, one within and the other outside the Cabinet. Unless a responsible Minister of a province has sufficient time to study the larger questions—which will only be possible if there is a sufficient number of Ministers—the scope for progress and development will be very limited, and suggestions from members of the Legislative Council may be inadequately met, or even resented.

All official proceedings should be regulated by precise rules and Acts, and should not depend merely upon the personal views and wishes of the officials. The whole system of official secrecy should be abolished.

Since, in future, the finances of provincial administrations will be separated from those of the Government of India, all payments, except the pensions of residents in the United Kingdom, should be made locally or through local agencies. The purchases for railways and Government institutions should also be made through local agencies, instead of through official channels, as at present.

Unless the re-constituted Government in each province is to adopt an entirely new policy, the reforms will prove barren of results. Under the old regime, the maintenance of order was the chief concern of the administration. Henceforward progress must be the watchword.

In preparing a programme of provincial reconstruction, one is faced with the initial difficulties presented by lack of homogeneity within the provinces, and by provincial variations. No attempt has been made to ensure that the provinces shall be approximately of the same area and population, nor even that each province will form a racial and linguistic unit. The following table shows at a glance some of these provincial variations :—

	Sq. miles.	Population.
Assam	53,015	6,713,635
Bengal	78,699	45,483,077
Bihar and Orissa .	83,181	34,490,084
Bombay	123,059	19,672,642
Central Provinces .	99,823	13,916,308
Madras	142,330	41,405,404
Punjab	99,779	19,974,956
United Provinces .	107,267	47,182,044

The new Government of India Act makes specific provision for the constitution of new provinces or sub-provinces. The Joint Select Committee did not think that any changes in the boundaries of a province should be made without due consideration of the views of the Legislative Council of that province. They were, however, of opinion that if the majority of the members of a Legislative Council representing a distinctive racial or linguistic territorial unit were to request that a separate province or sub-province be constituted, the Secretary of State should appoint a commission of inquiry, even though the majority of the Legislative Council of the province in question may be opposed to such a scheme.

The provinces should be reconstituted so that none of them may have a population of less than 10,000,000 nor more than 25,000,000 persons. A smaller unit is likely to be so weak as to find it difficult to resist the pressure of the Central Government, nor will it be able to command the resources to provide on a sufficiently large scale institutions and associations such as Universities, and departments of industry, commerce, agriculture and co-operative societies, necessary for rapid development.

In the forefront of the reconstruction problems should be put the expansion of the urban populations, the extension and improvement of educational facilities and economic development. The problems are interrelated and interdependent. More urban population is essential for carrying on the work of civilization. Without increasing the urban population it will be impossible to relieve the soil of the pressure under which it is groaning or to have economic development on a large scale. Similarly, any real advance in social and material progress is impossible without more and better education.

The following figures show how small indeed is the urban population in India as compared with other countries :—

	Per cent.
England	75
Canada	48
United States	55
Japan	49
India	10

Without considerable increase of urban population in the immediate future, it will be impossible for India to expand her industries, trade and commerce on a scale that will enable her to hold her own in the world. The economic interests will not be sufficiently safeguarded until the urban population is at least doubled.

It is to be hoped that the elected Council in each province will be able to induce Government to provide sufficient funds and establishments to stimulate enterprise in these directions. It is, indeed, imperative that money be found for this purpose, no matter what sacrifices may be involved. As large a proportion as possible of current provincial revenues should be set apart, and for any balance that may be needed, loans, earmarked for educational and industrial development, should be raised in each province. This proposal is further elaborated in the chapter on "Finance."

The Joint Select Committee suggested the creation of a Local Government Board for each province with a view to developing local self-government in cities, towns and rural areas. The new department, when constituted, should study the local government schemes of the Dominions and Japan before preparing its own plans. The new Municipal Act of Ontario (Canada) especially deserves careful consideration.

The time is ripe for the grant of complete self-government to local bodies, with powers of borrowing for local productive undertakings. No doubt, at the outset, some local bodies may misuse their powers or make mistakes. Wisdom in such matters can, however, only be acquired in the hard school of experience. Fortunately, each governing body will be self-contained and, therefore, the evil effects of any mistakes that may be made need not extend beyond the area directly concerned. Practice in local self-government should enable the people better to grasp the constructive issues involved in the more responsible spheres of provincial and national government.

Every means should be employed to increase the resources of the districts and sub-districts. Local corporations should undertake the construction of small tanks, canals, communications, including railways, and other works of public utility, the public interests being safeguarded, where necessary, by Provincial Acts and Charters. The formation of these corporations would provide practical work for the population, and would confer the greatest benefit on a district, especially if the capital was raised, and all the directors, experts and artisans were recruited, locally.

At the beginning it may be necessary to obtain experts from outside, but if the control and direction be in the hands of the district authorities, the work would constitute a source of practical education to the people, who have hitherto lacked such opportunities for training. Enterprises of this description, besides increasing production, will stimulate local patriotism and self-help.

The development of productive works and public utilities will immediately provide the Indian Ministers with great scope for remunerative enterprise. An irrigation scheme, for instance, which may cost, say, a crore of rupees, may, under favourable conditions, add the gross value of a crore to the annual productive yield, in addition to returning interest on the capital expended.

Although electricity comes under the head of "reserved subjects" there is no reason why hydro-electric works should not be developed by Indian agency with expert advisers. This has been done very successfully in Mysore.

The larger public works should be under national ownership, and their construction should be undertaken by indigenous agencies, while their subsequent management should be under public control.

The Joint Select Committee suggested that standing committees of the Legislative Council be appointed in each province and attached to the more important Government departments. Presumably this plan will be adopted when the new constitution becomes fully operative. In addition, independent commissions will be needed to help to solve some of the larger problems of provincial administration.

If we are to make substantial progress, no time should be lost in preparing for the task that lies before us. Civics and elementary economics should form subjects for instruction in schools of all grades. Every city, town and village should have some sort of public association to spread knowledge of the various systems of responsible government practised by the self-governing Dominions and other constitutionally governed countries.

It will conduce greatly to the success of the effort to provide adequate training in industry, trade and education, if the provincial Governments arrange to send deputations of local merchants, business men and educationists to countries like Canada, Japan and Australia, to learn the technical processes and methods of development employed there.

An annual review of the work done to develop the capacity of the people and the country's resources should be discussed in every Legislative Council, and issued with Government authority. The various public bodies should also issue reports of their own activities so that the views of all parties engaged in speeding up the progress of the provinces may be available.

Committees composed of officials and non-officials should be constituted in the districts, and even in the sub-districts, for the discussion of public questions. Even though these bodies will be of a purely advisory character, they will help to bring the executive into close touch with the people—a close touch which at present is entirely lacking. Through such intercourse the officials will lose their attitude of isolation and domination, and the people that awe of authority which is peculiar to India and stands in the way of co-operation and progress.

An Indian who has travelled in foreign countries is struck with the difference between the official attitude towards the people in those lands and in India. Whereas in other countries officials regard themselves as public servants and make it easy for the public to approach them, in India far too many officials look upon themselves as rulers, and make approach difficult. This criticism, it is to be feared, applies with almost as much force to Indian as to British officials.

An Indian who has travelled abroad is also likely to be struck with the contrast offered by the dispatch with which official work is performed in other countries as compared with the practice in India. Letters which, in other lands, would be answered the day they are received, in India remain unanswered in an office for days and even for weeks. Matters which would be decided finally in the course of a few days in any progressive country are hung up in India for weeks and even for months. Legal delays are especially vexatious.

Much could be accomplished by simplifying the administrative routine. Much also could be accomplished by regulating the hours of work and the holidays. At present the officials do not begin work until 11 a.m., and that in a hot country where the early morning is the best time for work. They also stop work much earlier than do people in other countries. As to public holidays, no country comes anywhere near the Indian prodigality in that respect. In all these matters, the standards should be made to approximate to those prevailing in progressive countries.

While no effort is neglected to make institutions fit in with local exigencies, the provinces, as far as possible, should be developed on a uniform basis. Indian national solidarity is the object to be aimed at. Any accentuation of provincial differences will cut at the root of nationhood.

CHAPTER V

LOCAL SELF-GOVERNMENT

"LOCAL self-government has been described by a political philosopher as that 'system of government under which the greatest number of minds, knowing the most, and having the fullest opportunities of knowing it, about the special matter in hand, and having the greatest interest in its well-working, have the management of it, or control over it.' Centralization has been described as that 'system of government under which the smallest number of minds, or those knowing the least, and having the fewest opportunities of knowing it, about the special matter in hand, and having the smallest interest in its well-working, have the management of it, or control over it.' An immense amount of wretched misgovernment might have been avoided, according to John Fiske, if all Legislators and all voters had those two wholesome maxims engraven upon their minds."

These words, quoted from an article by Mr. Henry Wade Rogers in the *North American Review*, 1908, indicate the value attached to local self-government by many leading Western minds.

"The writers on political institutions," he says further, "have . . . taught us that under local self-government officials exist for the benefit of the people, and that under centralization the people exist for the benefit of the official; that local self-government provides for the political education of the people, and centralization, based upon the principle that everything is to be done for the people rather than by the people, creates a spirit of dependence which dwarfs the intellectual and moral faculties and incapacitates for citizenship; . . . that the basis of local self-government is confidence in the people, while the fundamental idea of centralization is distrust of the people."

Whilst not necessarily accepting these words without qualification, it is well worth while for every Indian to weigh and consider them carefully in the light of his own country's situation.

Most cities and many of the smaller towns of British India at present possess a limited measure of self-government; but, as stated in the Montagu-Chelmsford Report, the local bodies have had little freedom in the higher spheres of administration and finance. No attempt has been made to introduce an efficient system of self-government in local areas either on the British or other foreign model, or to increase the urban population.

The smallness of expenditure by municipal and district boards is another evidence of the low level of their activities. In 1917–18, the municipal boards in all cities and towns spent less than £8,500,000, and the expenditure of rural boards, charged with the duty of meeting the rural needs of a population exceeding

220,000,000 persons, amounted to only about £7,600,000.

In rural areas special taxes for local purposes are levied on minor industries, vehicles, animals, etc., besides a sur-tax on land revenue. In most parts of the country the proceeds are mainly spent upon district roads, ferries, medical institutions and the like, and the establishments maintained for the purpose. Little or nothing is allocated to meet the local needs of the villages which actually pay the taxes.

One of the most important duties which the reconstituted Government in each province will be called upon to perform will be to survey the field of local activities, study foreign experience, and pass a liberal measure of self-government suited to the peculiar conditions of the province. A Local Government Board will, no doubt, be created in each province under the new measure. The future progress of the country will depend upon the manner in which the new administration discharges this responsibility, for only by a thorough-going process of district life can scope be provided for popular initiative and the work of development accelerated. Active participation in local affairs will also train the people to administer their provincial and national affairs.

In view of the fact that nine-tenths of the people in India live in villages, it is necessary that the new scheme of local self-government should not be confined to districts and sub-districts, but should extend to the remotest hamlets, to discipline and stimulate rural life all over the country. A system of village government is urgently needed to provide roads, water supply, irrigation, drainage, etc., and to introduce sanitary regulation and order in the villages.

Many of the villages consist almost entirely of mud-built and thatched houses, and are so badly kept that they are little better than slums. The residents of villages lack social and political power, and have no effective means of civic union with their fellows to enable them to improve their condition by joint effort. Unless a proper system of village administration is introduced, local self-government will have no meaning to the vast rural population.

The authors of the Montagu-Chelmsford Report seemed to favour the revival of the *panchayets*, which, owing to centralization of administration, have decayed. They were, however, not quite sure that a satisfactory scheme can be created "out of the present uneven materials." They have, therefore, left the question of village government to be dealt with by the reconstituted provincial governments.

What should be the unit of rural self-government? "The Village" will be the answer which will most readily suggest itself. It has, however, to be recognized that many villages in India contain a population of less than 500 persons and, therefore, an individual village by itself is incapable of providing for local needs according to anything like civilized standards.

If, however, the individual village is too small a unit, the sub-district (*taluk*) into which villages are grouped for administrative purposes, is much too large for the cultivator to take an intelligent personal interest in local affairs. It is, therefore, necessary to find an intermediate unit, which, while large enough to possess resources adequate to provide for local needs, will not be so large as to obscure that personal, intimate interest, without which local administration can never be a success.

Japan, faced with a similar problem, has solved it by grouping some 72,000 small villages for purposes of local administration into about 12,000 unions. By this method, the remotest village has been enabled to attain to a standard of local education, production, sanitation and communications, which would have been beyond its capacity had it sought independently to meet such requirements.

Each union contains, as a rule, from 3,000 to 4,000 persons. Now and again, however, a group has a combined population as small as 1,000, or as large as 30,000 persons.

One of the model unions which the writer visited during his recent tour in Japan, consisted of five hamlets or villages. It was about twenty-four square miles in area, and had a population of 5,493 persons. It comprised ten divisions, and had fifty sub-divisions or groups of dwellings. The union, as a whole, had a headman or Soncho. Each division and sub-division had, in addition, its own headman.

The Soncho was elected by the people of the union subject to confirmation by the Governor of the prefecture (a section of the country corresponding to the Indian district). He was assisted in his duties by a council, composed of the divisional and sub-divisional headmen, elected by the people, and the officials. The people were usually guided by the decisions and advice of the council, special committees being appointed to settle disputes.

In many villages, separate councils are not appointed, but the Soncho, or elected headman, administers the affairs of the village with the aid of the village officials during the intervals between which the village assembly meets. The village assembly passes the budget and records its decisions, which are afterwards amplified and given effect to by the village council, when there is one, or by the village headman and his staff.

That council constituted a working committee of the union assembly, and formed a channel of communication between the union and the executive officer of the sub-district, who was in constant touch with the head of the prefecture. The latter, in turn, was in communication with the Central Government. The Government was thus able to understand the needs and answer the call of the remotest hamlet in the empire.

The village union is a political entity. Neither the Central Government nor the prefecture (district) authorities interfere with the work of the unions, but on the contrary, make generous contributions towards the development of their industrial and social life and send experts to advise them. At the time of the writer's last visit to Japan, seventy-five village unions were in receipt of special subsidies for exemplary work in local government.

The system of grouping villages for purposes of local administration which has been described, could be easily adapted to Indian conditions, without interfering with any of the existing arrangements for the collection of revenue or the maintenance of order in rural areas. A block of 250 villages included, say, in a sub-district, may be merged into forty or fifty unions, each union, or group, consisting of, on an average, five or six villages, and having the most central village as the head-quarters of the union. Even ten or twelve thinly populated hamlets might form one union, while a village with a population of 3,000 or more may stand by itself, and should be permitted to remain a unit of self-government.

All the villages comprised in a union would elect a council of seven to twelve members. The council should have two committees—one to attend to routine business, and the other to carry on work of development.

The union council may collect taxes and voluntary contributions of labour, and utilize them for improving roads and cart-tracks, drainage, water supply, irrigation, planting trees, and provide for lighting or such other needs and conveniences as their joint resources can supply. The field for self-improvement in this way is limited only by the energy, intelligence and activity of the people and their capacity for co-operative effort.

The villages may at first be reluctant to pay taxes for local improvements, but when they come to realize that the money is spent locally for their own benefit, they will not grudge meeting the demand. This especially will be the case when they find that the expenditure of money on local improvements leads to greater production and to improved conditions of living.

The duties of the village council would be regulated by the Acts of the Provincial Legislative Council, but there would be numerous other activities and wants which would have to be provided for by unofficial organizations. Ordinarily, every union should have primary and vocational schools, a village hall or meeting-place, reading rooms, libraries, agricultural and co-operative societies, a society for promoting rural public works, rural manufactures, study clubs, hotels and inns, young men's associations, and other social and civic organizations.

These or any other institutions that may be wanting should be gradually brought into existence through the co-operation of the village council and local unofficial organizations. The whole question of organization is dealt with in a later chapter.

Only by some such system of village government would it be possible to revive the instinct of self-help and self-improvement which has been lost through long disuse, and to place the Indian village on the road to health, comfort and prosperity.

According to the census of India, a city is a residential area containing a population of 20,000 persons or more. The larger and more prosperous the area, the greater will be its opportunities and activities and the resources at its disposal to provide for local needs according to modern requirements.

The administration of a city is entrusted to a municipal council, which will be subject to the provisions of the Local Self-Government Act, and to the general rules prescribed by the Local Government Board. That council should have (1) a managing committee, and (2) an improvement board. The executive committee should maintain roads, water supply, drainage, parks and other public utilities, while the improvement committee should prepare and execute plans for all new works and improvements. The latter committee should collect information as to how city work is carried on in progressive countries, and disseminate such information among the public to secure their interest and co-operation.

One important duty of the improvement committee would be to prepare schemes for town-planning, following, as far as possible, the English town-planning models, consistent with the limited resources of Indian cities. Residential and industrial suburbs should be laid out, with a view to providing suitable sites for houses and for the establishment of factories and workshops needed to provide occupations to a city population.

Unofficial agencies will be required to attend to civic needs which may fall outside the purview of duties of the municipal council.

A city should have a municipal hall and offices, libraries and reading-rooms, a commercial and industrial museum, an inquiry office, and a sufficiency of hotels, restaurants and inns. As in Canada, some cities might assume entire control over technical and commercial education.

Industry, commerce and banking should be specially encouraged, so that the city may become the centre of production and distribution for the neighbourhood. The necessary organizations such as a chamber of commerce, manufacturers', agricultural and bankers' associations and trade guilds for improving the economic life of the people, will be also needed. City organization would not be complete without reform societies, civic clubs, child welfare, and other public service organizations.

In Britain and in the United States systematic civic surveys are made from time to time to investigate the conditions of the city and to suggest suitable measures of amelioration. These surveys deal not only with material needs, but also take stock of "the common life and institutions, and the tone and spirit of the people." Every city in India should be subject to such a survey, which should include vital statistics, education, production, distribution of population according to occupations, trade, sanitation, public health, recreation and air spaces, housing, industrial conditions, charities, etc. Such surveys are best carried out by the citizens qualified for the work, aided by experts, and the results placed before the city authority and the residents of the city for discussion and action.

Places containing 5,000 to 20,000 persons are regarded by the census authorities in India as towns. The town occupies a position midway between the city and the village. Town administrative bodies and public organizations will, therefore, occupy a position midway between those of the village union and the city.

The town council should have (1) a managing committee and (2) an improvement board with functions similar to those of the city committees already described. There is abundant work in every town for improvement boards. Sufficient provision is not made as yet in many towns for their elementary needs, according to modern standards, in respect of roads, water supply and drainage.

The local affairs of the district may in future be administered by district Assemblies and district Boards, the former consisting of representatives from the village unions and towns in the district. The district Assemblies should elect the members of the Board, one-third of the members being re-elected every year.

The Board will be the chief executive authority for all local works and affairs. Under the direction of the Board, or its committees, a secretary and executive staff will attend to the administration of local matters in the district, such as rural education, roads, cart-tracks, bridges, water supply, drainage, veterinary work, sanitation, medical control, etc.

The Board and its staff will be maintained from the local funds of the district, contributed by the municipalities and village unions in the area, supplemented, where necessary, by special rates and contributions from the Provincial Government. The local taxes may be collected by the villages themselves, and a percentage of the proceeds, fixed by law, handed over for the expenses of the district Board. Special cesses may be levied for the purpose of constructing local works such as railways, tramways, road bridges, irrigation channels, and similar improvements, if the people of the locality who need them are willing to pay for them, the cesses being recovered from those who derive benefit from them.

One of the chief duties of the district Boards will be the development of local resources and communications. Works carried out for the purpose may, in addition to benefiting the people of the locality concerned, form a source of income to the district Board itself. There is abundant scope for developments of this character.

The construction of local works should, as far as possible, be entrusted to the people of the district, and the contracts given to corporations and companies formed in the area, with a view to affording training in business management, finding occupation for the people, and developing their executive capacity.

The work of the district Board may be carried on by two committees: one to concern itself with administration, and the other with formulating and executing development and improvement programmes.

Ordinarily, the local work of the sub-district (*taluk*) may be carried out by officials appointed by the district Board. Separate sub-district Boards may, however, be established where the area or population is large. Such a Board will differ from the district Board only in degree and not in organization and duties. Where a sub-district is established, the district Board will be relieved of its responsibility for the work of the *taluk*, except in the matter of co-ordinating that work with the rest of the district.

The district Assembly, already referred to, may meet once in three months to discuss the wants and needs of the district, to exchange views with the provincial officials and to pass the budgets of the district Board. The district Board will be responsible for giving effect to the decisions and resolutions passed by the Assembly in matters which pertain to the work of the Board.

The district Assembly should serve also as a consultative body to help the provincial Government to carry on the work of the district. It might appoint committees to advise the district officials, either in regard to general affairs, or for any special or individual developments that may be in progress between any two sessions of the Assembly.

For economic and other developments, committees of the district Assemblies may be constituted to advise officials of the departments concerned. The officials will also be present at the quarterly or other meetings of the district Assembly. Both the district Board and the district officers should be required to assist private organizations, and citizens' societies started for the purpose of training the people for responsible government, inculcating the idea of good citizenship and promoting culture, patriotism, discipline and thrift. It is hoped that in future provincial ministers and district officers will send advice and exhortations to the people from time to time, through the district Assemblies, as to the manner in which they should conduct themselves and co-operate with the provincial authorities in the work of local improvement and development.

Leaders of public opinion should begin at once to make a careful study of foreign systems of self-government, and should start special journals to popularize models suited to Indian conditions and to educate the public. The people should abandon the idea once for all that development will come in the course of time without study, preparation, effort, or the expenditure of money, and should be prepared to pay taxes and to make sacrifices.

Future developments in this respect will depend largely upon the character of the new scheme of local self-government to be introduced by the reformed provincial Governments, and upon the constitution and duties of the new Local Government Board to be established in each province.

CHAPTER VI

FINANCE

Many anomalies exist in the administration of India's finances.[1]

The annual budget is prepared both in pounds sterling and in rupees, although the latter is the standard unit of value in the country. A large sum, at present amounting to about £29,000,000, is annually budgeted for expenditure in the United Kingdom—mainly for military services, pensions and the purchase of stores.

Other countries, the Dominions not ex-

[1] The rates of exchange generally prevailing at the outbreak of the War have been adopted throughout the book. On this basis the rupee (16 annas) is fixed at 16*d.*, and 15 rupees go to £1 sterling.

A lakh of rupees (100,000) = £6,666 13*s.* 4*d.*; a crore of rupees (10 millions) = £666,666 13*s.* 4*d.*

The yen is about 2*s.* 0½*d.*, so that 2 yen roughly= 3 rupees. The American dollar is converted roughly at $4.85 to £1 sterling.

cepted, make payments through banks for expenditure incurred abroad. They purchase the necessary stores within the country itself through local firms.

Silver continues to be the internal currency of India—though many years ago an official committee recommended the establishment of a gold standard for India, and though gold is the standard accepted in all civilized countries. While the British sovereign is legal tender in India, there is no corresponding legal obligation in the United Kingdom to recognize the rupee, nor has there been any serious attempt to make the rupee convertible into gold in India at all times.

British trade with India is not left to follow its own course, but by means of council bills, telegraphic transfers and reverse drafts is financed through the Secretary of State. The gold exchange and paper currency reserves, running into something like £100,000,000, are held in London instead of being retained in India to promote Indian credit and to help Indian trade, and loans at low rates of interest are made therefrom to British traders. It has been truly said that the Secretary of State is both the ruler and banker of India.

All departments of Indian finance are inter-penetrated by the influence of British trade. As Lord Bryce says :—

> "The more any public authority or any National Government either itself undertakes or interferes with the conduct by private persons of any matter in which money can be either made or spent, the more grounds does it supply the private persons for trying to influence its action in the direction which will benefit such persons."[1]

If this occurs in a National Government the evil effects in a dependency will be far greater.

The financiers with whom the writer has discussed the question consider the system of finance followed in India as highly prejudicial to Indian interests. Under an effective international currency, that is, gold, all the Indian money would go back to India and be available for expansion of credit there, so as to benefit Indian

[1] *The Hindrances to Good Citizenship*, by Lord Bryce, p. 45.

trade and industry. The present conditions of exchange in Europe and America make it imperative for India to adopt an effective gold standard. In normal times, the balance of trade has in most years been in favour of India, so that an effective gold standard was always a practicable scheme.

During the War, on account of her dependent position, the monetary affairs of India were controlled from London. The people suffered from high prices. The war profits went to a very small percentage of business men. Many commodities were purchased very much below the world prices. Food control was exercised secretly, without the public being aware of the extent to which food was exported. Great mortality was caused through lack of proper sustenance during the influenza epidemic. The export of articles such as hides was controlled in order to secure them for Britain and her Allies below the market value. In order to maintain artificial conditions of exchange, ordinary trade in rice, jute, timber, wheat, hides and other articles was prohibited on private account, and in some cases stopped. India lost heavily on her investments in England, and her own money in the currency reserves remained locked up in England. Large purchases of silver were made through commercial agencies instead of in India itself.

A self-governing Dominion would, while all the time loyally helping Great Britain, have greatly added to her own wealth. Canada, as one of her statesmen told the writer, in spite of the sacrifices she made for the War, is at present "rolling in wealth." Japan and the United States have immensely strengthened their economic and financial position. The United States is now leading the world both in trade and finance, and is the only free gold market of to-day. The War gave Japan the opportunity which foreign competition had withheld from her. Under capable Indian, or even pro-Indian, management, India's economic position could have been immensely strengthened, and what she lost within the last fifty years might have been restored to her during the five years of the War.

The large sums of money annually budgeted for military expenditure are difficult to justify, especially when it is remembered that India is a dependent and not an independent country.

In the budget for the year 1920–21, £41,000,000 has been set aside for purposes of defence. This amounts to nearly half the total net revenue of the country. Military expenditure on such a scale in peace time is without parallel in any country in the world. Britain spent much less on her army in pre-war times. Even the Japanese Empire spends only a fraction of this sum.

In view of the altered conditions, the whole military and naval expenditure and defence organization of the country must be placed on a new basis. This work should be entrusted to a commission comprising an adequate number of Indians, as soon as reasonably possible after the reformed government comes into being.

The report of the Esher Committee on Indian Army Reform just issued (October, 1920) reveals the dangers to which Indian finance and the Indian constitution is exposed in the future. Even the London "Times" considers the report very extraordinary since in a sense the proposals amount to handing over the army in India, and half the Indian imperial expenditure, to the direct control of the British War Office. Under the scheme, all the Indians have to do is to find the money. One wonders what a Dominion government would say if such a proposal were placed before it.

Lord Macaulay stated in 1833 when the East India Company's Charter was renewed for the last time, that the Indian revenue was larger than that of any country in the world except France. That position no longer exists, though since then large and populous tracts of territory have been added to the Indian Empire.

While, during the twenty years ending 1913–14, the revenue in India increased by about 36 per cent., during the same period it expanded 115 per cent. in the United Kingdom, 245 per cent. in Canada, and 640 per cent. in Japan. These figures, sufficiently accurate to serve as a basis of comparison, show that while those countries have been making rapid progress, India has practically stood still.

Canada, with a population of a little over 8,000,000 persons, yielded a revenue of more than £34,000,000 in 1916, or £45,000,000 including provincial revenue. With a population thirty times as large, British India yielded only double that amount. But whereas Canada has been free to develop her resources, India has been in leading strings.

Though the increase of revenue is small, the administration is costly, and its demands are constantly growing.

The sources from which the Government of India derives its revenue have certain distinctive features due to India's position as a dependency. In the United Kingdom, for instance, the principal sources of revenue are customs, excise, estate duties, property and income-tax, posts, telegraphs, etc. In the United States they are excise, licences and other internal revenues, customs, postal revenue, etc. In Canada they are customs, excise, public works, and income-tax (during the War). In India, on the other hand, customs revenue and income-tax have been kept very low. The sheet-anchor of Indian finance, to use the phrase of a finance member of the Government of India, is land-tax, which is drawn from the poorest of the poor, and amounts to about £22,000,000.

Indian revenue can easily be doubled in ten years and trebled in fifteen if a satisfactory policy for the development of education and of production from industries and agriculture is adopted, and many of the restrictive influences incidental to the position of a dependency are removed.

Another unique point in respect of Indian finance is that the entire proceeds from all the provinces are swept into the central treasury, and sums doled out to the provinces, not according to the demands or needs of the population, but according to the wishes of the Central Government or of the India Office, because the Secretary of State in Council determines all the appropriations of the Government of India. The discussion of the Budget in provincial

Councils, or even in the Imperial Council, has, therefore, been futile, and no real opportunity has been afforded to initiate large economic or social experiments in any of the provinces.

Orders have now been issued to separate provincial from central finance. The manner in which effect is being given to the orders so far cannot, however, be regarded as satisfactory, since the complete separation of finance is not being insisted upon. Nor has any attempt been made to readjust, on an equitable basis, the contributions levied from the various provinces by the Government of India. Madras and the United Provinces, though both economically weak, are most unfairly treated, and this injustice is to continue.

The central revenues should be restricted to a few specific imposts such as customs, net income from railways and income-tax. As a cardinal principle of finance, the whole field of taxation, excepting those few taxes levied by the Central Government, should be in the hands of Provincial Governments.

The gross railway revenue and expenditure as entered in the budget swells the figures in a misleading manner.

The railways should be carried on by the Government through indigenous agencies, to be trained at once for this purpose, and administered in the interests of the population, and not, as at present, merely in the interests of Government revenue.

The separation of provincial finance will ensure that money raised locally will be spent locally. That will inspire confidence in the tax-payer—confidence which will make it possible to collect more revenue in the provinces, as experience has proved in the United States and Canada.

Cities and towns should be permitted to contract loans, subject to recognized restrictions, for public utilities and productive works, if the interest charges and sinking-funds can be met from local taxes and rates.

If the system of grouping villages for purposes of local administration, recommended in the preceding chapter, is adopted it would be easy to develop a satisfactory scheme of rural finance. After meeting the urgent current expenditure on sanitation, repair and maintenance of roads and lighting, the balance available should be devoted to :—

(1) Education.
(2) Local improvements ; and
(3) Measures necessary to train the people, and to improve the economic and social condition of the poorest among them.

The principle of making the locality raise half the money needed for education and other development purposes, and obtaining the other half by provincial grants, may answer well for most provinces for the present.

The division of revenue between the central, provincial and local authorities leaves much to be desired. In 1914, for instance, the imperial and provincial expenditure in India was £85,000,000 ; district and sub-district expenditure, £3,900,000 ; municipal, £5,400,000 ; making a total of £94,300,000. In Japan the corresponding figures were £59,000,000, £8,000,000, £21,000,000, and a total of £88,000,000 respectively. Whatever the discrepancy in the basis of comparison, the statistics are accurate enough to show that the local expenditure in Japan is very much greater than it is in India, notwithstanding the fact that the rural population of India is much larger.

Calculations made upon the basis of rough estimates of gross annual income before the War, show that taxation in India bears a higher proportion to the income of the tax-payer than it does in most civilized countries. In the United Kingdom, for instance, the gross annual income before the War was estimated at about £2,300,000,000, and the national expenditure at about £200,000,000, or less than one-eleventh. For India the corresponding figures were £600,000,000 and £83,000,000, or a little over one-seventh.

According to the late Mr. Justice Ranade, who for a long time administered the Deccan Agriculturists Relief Act under the Bombay Government, the land-tax encroaches upon the profits and wages of the poor peasant, who has to accommodate himself to a low standard of life with every increase of economic pressure on his class. In the case of smaller payments, the land-tax interferes with the means of subsistence, and in the case of larger ones it discourages agricultural development. From whatever point of view it is considered, the tax in its present form is harmful.

The taxable incomes in most countries are reckoned upon people's earnings after deducting whatever is needed for a fair subsistence allowance. The finances in civilized countries are tending towards complete exemption from taxation of all persons whose incomes fall below a certain minimum. If such a test were applied to the Indian cultivator, a great majority of his class would not be liable to pay any tax at all. But the land-tax can be adjusted only when a more equitable system of taxation has been made possible by economic developments.

As regards excise from alcoholic drinks, which is a considerable source of revenue at present in India, it is desirable to aim at its abolition as quickly as possible, because it is derived by encouraging vice among the people.

The United States has "gone dry," and

the Canadian Provinces are following the example. Scotland has lately begun voting upon local option. There is in England a strong movement in favour of this reform. Why should not India, where the higher classes are not addicted to drink, be permitted to ban liquor by means of a similar process, gradual enough to permit the necessary financial readjustment to take place?

Since national exigencies demand the development of education and industries at an unprecedented rate, and since, for some years, it is not possible to provide, out of current revenue, the large sums needed for the purpose, it is necessary that a loan averaging about fifteen crores per annum be raised for these purposes during the next ten years.

A loan for education is unusual, but so are India's conditions. The Japanese Government has not hesitated recently to float a loan for education, though great educational progress has already been made, and though the Diet opposed the loan on the ground that education was not a business transaction nor a productive public work. In India, the position is exactly the reverse. The people's representatives have been clamouring for more and better education, and the Government has been pleading financial inability, though that did not prevent it from incurring a substantial amount of unproductive war debt. An addition of at least an equal amount (133 crores) for education, industries, and other development purposes could hardly be regarded as piling up unproductive debt.

Each province may be permitted to raise money internally. If credit and confidence are established, there is no reason why these internal loan operations should not prove successful.

The public debt of India is made up as follows :—

	Crores of Rupees.
Ordinary war debt	133
Productive railways	359
Irrigation	66
Total	558

To this will have to be added in future, as stated above, a yearly loan of fifteen crores for ten years to come. Such increase, in addition to any increase in taxation, will be cheerfully faced by the people, if they are sure that the proceeds will be applied strictly to the purposes mentioned.

As currency and banking will be dealt with in a later chapter, it is here necessary only to draw attention to the great importance of establishing a federal banking system with a central control, giving India an effective gold standard and separating Indian finance from British trade with India. Similarly, as the subject of fiscal autonomy will be treated later, it is merely necessary to state here that the true basis of Indian progress will be established if the India Office control of the Indian finances ceases, if payment of "home charges" is made through the London branch of the Indian Central Bank or banking system, and if India is permitted to redistribute the incidence of taxation and expand her finances as suits her best. Fiscal reconstruction should be the corner-stone of the economic and social edifice of the future.

The entire subject of Indian finance needs to be impartially investigated, if for no other reason than to remove the suspicion entertained by well-informed unprejudiced persons who believe that financial anomalies have been permitted to grow up in order to preserve British monopoly over the Indian trade and hold Indian gold in London. A commission for that purpose should be appointed as early as possible. It should be composed of two-thirds Indian representatives, and the remaining one-third of experts and officials. The commission should be permitted to appoint its own staff and to carry on direct correspondence with the Dominions and foreign countries, and to submit recommendations. It seems desirable that such a commission should be appointed at once, and maintained for four or five years, until the finances are all brought into a condition, as near as circumstances allow, to that of Canada or Australia, because only by placing the Indian finances upon a Dominion basis can the anomalies which exist be eliminated.

The currency policy should hereafter be settled by the Government of India with the approval of the Indian Legislature and Indian public opinion. There should be no delay, therefore, in the establishment of a commission for five years, and of a permanent financial committee of the Central Legislative Assembly and similar bodies in each province, as suggested. Experts and officials, though represented on these central and provincial legislative committees, should have no power to vote. It is to be hoped that, in future, there may be complete open dealing and publicity in regard to all money transactions.

Economic Reconstruction

CHAPTER VII

ECONOMIC ACTIVITIES IN ADVANCED COUNTRIES

Now that a measure of self-government has been vouchsafed to India, and the Joint Select Committee has clearly stated "that she should have the same liberty to consider her" fiscal "interests as Great Britain or any self-governing Dominion," it should be easy to reconstruct her trade and industry, and to develop her natural resources in a manner not hitherto possible.

The lines on which economic reconstruction should proceed will be better understood if a rapid survey is made of the methods pursued in the United Kingdom, Canada, the United States of America and Japan to increase production and to promote trade and industry.

Ever since the reorganization of the

national life for war purposes, there has been more vigorous thinking and more definite suggestions in regard to social experiment in Britain than, perhaps, in any other country. Not long after hostilities began, a committee on reconstruction was constituted. This was later converted into a department, which, if it did nothing else, issued a series of pamphlets containing much valuable information on various phases of reconstruction — information which needs to be carefully read in India, and adapted to Indian requirements.

Four broad economic tendencies are at present noticeable in Great Britain:

Firstly, the Government is taking direct action to secure maximum production in essential industries and to stimulate invention. The most important instances are the encouragement of agricultural production during the War, and the determined endeavour to occupy the first place in the matter of manufacturing dyes. With this is connected the realization, slower in England than in Germany and the United States of America, of the paramount value of scientific research in industry—as, for example, in the setting aside of a sum of a million sterling by the Department of Scientific and Industrial Research for grants in aid.

Secondly, the Government has been forced by clamorous need to assist local authorities and private enterprise in so fundamental a service as housing. Years before the War, it was becoming clear that the re-housing of the greater part of the population, especially the agricultural labourers, was an urgent problem which could be solved only by a comprehensive national policy. Since the War all doubts, even of the most convinced advocates of the policy of *laissez-faire,* have been swept away, and the Government has undertaken the task.

Thirdly, despite disinclination on the part of the present Ministry, there is an increasing trend of public opinion towards the State control of the essential national services, especially mines and transport. Nothing, it is evident, can check the growth of the enormous combines which are the distinctive economic characteristic of the age—in textiles, leather, oil, coal, steel and shipping.

As a result of the War, there have been many amalgamations of trade and business interests. At present five great combines do most of the banking in England.

Fourthly, the tendency towards the extension of public control and the workers' demand for an altered status is equally irresistible. No longer is it possible, with the transition from free competition to vast modern combines, for the community and the Government to be left out of the concern, while, on the other hand, the workers of every class and kind declare themselves emphatically against the continuance of a wage system divorced from responsibility in management. Four years ago, the first authoritative recognition of this development came with the report issued by the Whitley Committee, recommending joint industrial councils, upon which representatives of the workers and of the employers should sit together. Since the last year of the War, there has been a remarkable expansion of the Industrial Council movement, which is universally regarded as a first stage in the transfer of control. Of greater importance still is the development in railways and mines which is destined to lead, in a brief period, to entirely new forms of ownership and control.

An Imperial Trade Investigation Board has been set up, and a private British Trade Corporation has been established under Royal Charter with the express object of financing and developing foreign trade.

When so industrially advanced a country as Britain finds it necessary to make breaches in her policy of free trade, how can the policy of *laissez-faire* be continued in India, which is still in the agricultural stage ?

Canada, like India, is essentially an agricultural country, but while the Dominion authorities realize the futility of depending merely upon agriculture, effort is made to keep India agricultural. The latest figures for Canada [1] show that the total production from industries and manufactures exceeds that from agriculture. The volume of manufactured products, which are protected by a tariff duty averaging about 25 per cent., is constantly increasing. Banking is also advancing at a rapid rate, and a notable movement for international banking expansion has begun.

The Canadian Government has at the present time concentrated its attention upon increasing and extending foreign trade. The Department of Trade and Commerce, the most important national organization, and the Department of Finance and Banking are working assiduously to this end.

Attention is being given to the Commercial Intelligence Service, and large schemes have been projected for the encouragement of industries. All the public departments are energetic in preparing and circulating reports and bulletins. A weekly

[1] Current production, 1917 :—

	Dols.
Agriculture	1,621 millions.
Fishing	39 ,,
Forestry	175 ,,
Mining	190 ,,
Manufacturing . . .	2,400 ,,

bulletin with a large free circulation is issued by the Federal Government. Indeed, the Canadian Governments have set a standard in the matter of promoting industrial education and providing assistance through public agency and propaganda. The importance of such help cannot be exaggerated.

The Dominion Government deals chiefly with the survey service and foreign trade, while the actual work of exploiting national resources and giving assistance to business concerns is left to the Provincial Governments. A single province has recently made appropriations of nearly $2,000,000 for the establishment of new industries, and is prepared to lend dollar for dollar when private individuals and corporations signify their desire to start them. In eastern Canada municipalities grant facilities to encourage small industries.

The Indian practice stands in direct contrast to the Canadian standards. The Central and Provincial Governments in India are extremely chary of subsidizing any industry. There was in recent years at least one occasion on which orders went from London which in substance prohibited the active encouragement of industry.

In the United States of America, as in Canada, industries have been protected by a high tariff wall, though American industrialists, by their ability to combine, have been able to do without Government subsidies.

Americans have, of course, been greatly helped by the abundance of their resources. both in materials and in trained men. Industries have reached an adolescent stage, and many of them can safely dispense with protective duties.

Extensive use of labour-saving machinery and motive power and economic and efficient management of business distinguish American industry.

Huge industries and mammoth trusts have grown up.

For instance, the annual business of the Ford Motor Company at Detroit approximates $350,000,000. The average number of employees regularly on the pay roll is about 36,000. The plant turns out a complete motor-car every twenty-nine seconds and, in conjunction with its branch factories, has a record of 3,000 cars made in a single day of eight hours.

The wealth of individual citizens has risen to prodigious proportions. Mr. John D. Rockefeller's fortune is estimated at three billion dollars and his income at one hundred million dollars a year.

The banking work of America is carried on by 8,000 or 9,000 principal banks, each of which is a member of the Federal Reserve Bank of the district in which it is situated. There are twelve Federal Reserve Banks, controlled by a Federal Reserve Board at Washington. The Board has recently agreed to establish branch banks abroad, and there is a move in New York and Washington at present to help the Central and South American States to place their currencies on a gold basis.

Another characteristic of American business organization is the Chambers of Commerce or Boards of Trade established throughout the country. The Central

Chamber of Commerce of the United States comprises the combined forces of America's leading commercial organizations. It represents the body of American business men at the seat of the Federal Government at Washington, where it maintains an executive Board. Manufacturers and business men serve on its committees. It has a staff of experienced experts, conducts bureaux of administration, organization service, research, industrial relations and service to members, and has at its command an editorial staff with a national vision, and a field force to reach its nation-wide membership.

The reconstruction aims of the American nation at present, briefly stated, are: (1) increased production in industries and agriculture; (2) extension of foreign trade, and (3) increase of American shipping.

Americans have realized that shipping and all the correlated improvements pertaining to a merchant marine are necessary to the expansion of the general trade of the country. They have realized that lack of shipping has handicapped their foreign trade. Shipping is, therefore, receiving the largest amount of attention of both the Government and the people at the present time. In September, 1919, a prominent business man in New York, in course of conversation with the writer, remarked that the shipbuilding going on in the country over-shadowed every other activity. The coast is filled with shipbuilding yards. The biggest shipbuilding plant in the world is at Hog Island. Created as a war measure, it is now used for building merchant ships. Fifty ships can be built there at the same time.

Shipping is entirely under the control of the Shipping Board, which builds ships and sells them to private firms. America is convinced that where a great volume of tonnage is congregated, competition fixes the lowest rates.

Both Government and the people are doing their utmost to expand foreign trade. The Government is training at Washington a number of young men who, after passing an examination in exports and imports, are to be sent to European countries as trade agents, to foster export business. The Bureau of Foreign and Domestic Commerce disseminates the information received from its Trade Commissioners and foreign commercial Attachés, by means of reports, by a daily newspaper, and by the publication every month of statistical information, of which a summary is published annually.

A new plan adopted to stimulate foreign trade includes (1) moving pictures, to acquaint the people of other countries with American goods and manufactures; (2) the exhibition of foreign samples of machinery and manufactured products; and (3) a carefully classified collection of the documents used in foreign trade.

Since all industrial progress in Japan has been achieved in comparatively recent years, she offers to India the most direct and valuable lessons obtainable in material advancement and reconstruction.

In Japan direct relations exist between the Government and industry. There pioneer industries were, indeed, set going and, for years, maintained at the public cost.

Down to thirty years ago, for instance, the Government, as owner of shipyards, was able to give direct assistance and guaranteed dividends to chartered companies. A law passed at the close of the century was designed to encourage shipbuilding by means of Government subsidies of from 11 to 22 yen per ton. Great trade expansion resulted from this policy, and the shipbuilding industry became so firmly planted and prosperous that about ten years ago the Government was able to withdraw from active participation in it. Subsidies in the shape of fixed annual sums, however, are still granted to enable shipping lines to send vessels to fresh destinations. It is impossible to dispute the results of this policy. Before the War, Japan stood seventh among the maritime nations. To-day, she occupies the third place.

Among Japanese statesmen, the view prevails that the unifying effect of the wars with China and Russia was felt strongly and permanently in the field of collective and industrial effort. It is certainly true that the industries of Japan received an impetus from both conflicts.

Apart from such stimulus, the Japanese Government has set an example of consistent and continuous thought and action with a constructive social purpose. Research work is carried on at the Universities, chambers of commerce, societies and guilds in every large city, and, as far as possible, in the smaller towns, many of the associations having their duties fixed by law.

Two large experimental stations at Tokyo and Osaka work in close touch with manufacturers and are constantly engaged in experiments calculated to improve old industries and to advance new ones. Institutes of Science started by private companies are aided by Government and by the Imperial Household. The institutes of technology and the Universities give thorough instruction in mechanical and chemical engineering, and in economics.

In Japan, of course, industries are carried

on under protective tariffs ranging from twenty to sixty per cent.

The formation of voluntary industrial associations is encouraged by law. The erection of steelworks is encouraged by concessions of land and by special tax exemptions.

So also in the departments of banking and commerce. The authorities in Japan consider that the banking system of the country, which has been developed and perfected after a careful study of conditions in all foreign countries, is quite satisfactory. They maintain a central bank, viz., the Bank of Japan, as the apex of the system. This is the only note-issuing bank. Each prefecture has a private bank of its own, which does corresponding duty for the Government of the prefecture. The industries of the country are helped by a Central Industrial Bank, which is authorized by Government to issue bonds to the extent of ten times its paid-up capital. Agricultural banks give agricultural loans. The Yokohama Specie Bank, which is also helped by Government and which has numerous branch banks in foreign countries, is most useful to Japanese merchants doing business abroad.

The Japanese Government keeps in close touch with merchants and with the foreign markets, watching the supplies of raw materials and the openings for manufactured articles. There are from sixty to seventy chambers of commerce and thirty-seven commercial museums established by prefectures, districts and cities. At Harbin and at Singapore, similar institutions display, side by side, the products of Japan and those of competing nations. In the matter of trade agents and syndicates for the exploitation of markets outside their own country, the Japanese are certainly as alert and enterprising as any people in the West. Not only do they endeavour to keep in touch with the world's activities, but they work upon the principle that it is a good thing for Japan to take part, as far as may be, in every department of those activities.

Japanese embassies and consulates are notably energetic in collecting material and making reports. These are speedily placed at the disposal of the public—as often, indeed, as twice a week. Japanese merchants are encouraged to travel abroad. In 1916 the Japanese Government dispatched a commission of ten members to the United States. When such commissions are chosen by the Government of India, there is usually not an Indian on them.

Commercial students to the number of about eighty every year are sent out to foreign countries after being given such local equipment as may be possible. The system was started about twenty years ago and already nearly 600 experts and business men have been trained in this way.

The first lesson to be drawn from this survey by the Government and the people of India is that industries and trade do not grow of themselves, but have to be willed, planned and systematically developed. In none of the countries that have been named—certainly not in England, not even in *laissez-faire* America—has Government kept aloof from the industrial activities of the people. On the contrary, in the earlier stages and in the present developed condition alike, Government has entered energetically into the service of commerce and industry. This especially is the case in Japan, whose industrial policies India needs to adopt as far as possible, if she desires rapid progress.

In India, Government has shown some enterprise in developing railways and irrigation ; but the expansion of trade and industry has been a matter of British domination and has left the people of the country disinherited, with no share in the control of policy or its operation.

The times are rapidly and decisively changing. It is no more possible, to-day, for the industrial exploitation of India to continue without the participation of the Indian people themselves, than it is for the working people of Britain or the United States to return to their pre-war status.

CHAPTER VIII

TRADE AND COMMERCE

To understand the present position of India's foreign trade, it is necessary to compare the figures for the four years ending 1914 and 1918 respectively. During the four years ending 1914, the average annual exports amounted to £155,000,000 and imports to £106,000,000, representing an average total trade of £261,000,000. The corresponding figures for the four years ending 1918 were £146,000,000, £101,000,000 and £247,000,000 respectively.

If due allowance is made for the rise in prices between 1913–14 and 1917–18, which amounted to 111 per cent. for imports and 25 per cent. for exports, it will be seen that the volume of trade in the latter year was considerably less than may be inferred from the mere value.

The following table shows at a glance the effect of the War on India's foreign trade as compared with that of some of the principal countries of the world :—

Country.	Trade per head in 1913–14.	Trade per head in 1918–19.
	£	£
United Kingdom . .	30	40
Canada . . .	2·9	7
United States . .	8·8	18·4
India	·8	·8

In considering these figures it must be remembered that the price levels have altered in all the countries. The total value of Indian foreign trade in 1918–19 amounted to £282,000,000. The corresponding figures for Belgium in 1913 before the War, and for Canada in 1918 towards the end of the War, were £326,000,000 and £509,000,000, respectively. The population of Belgium in 1911 was 7,500,000 and of Canada 7,200,000, while India represented no less than 315,000,000.

During the War, while Canada increased her exports by 231 per cent. and Japan by 232 per cent., India's export trade showed no advance. The official report makes the complacent remark that in the matter of foreign trade in 1918, India yielded pride of place to Canada. Two nations, both within the British Empire, one with a population of 315,000,000 including the Indian States, and the other with less than 8,000,000, have about the same amount of foreign trade. While actively engaged in the War, Canada increased her industrial activities and output, whereas India made little or no progress.

Civilized nations the world over attach great importance to trade as an index to national prosperity. The War is over, and the international trade competition termed "war after the War" has begun. It would be extremely suicidal if Indians failed to make a special effort, at this juncture, to take part in the industrial and trade activities of the world. India's competition in the world market is not the only question involved. If Indian industries are not rapidly developed, the Indian market itself is in danger of being permanently captured by foreign nations. Increased production in India is necessary both in agriculture and in manufactures, particularly the latter, so that home as well as foreign trade may be increased.

The so-called foreign trade of India outside Bombay is in the hands of British and foreign merchants. Very little of it is in the hands of the Indians themselves.

The principal exports from India are food products and raw materials fit for manufactures, whereas in economically advanced countries they chiefly consist of manufactured articles. Imports into India consist principally of manufactured articles, more than half of which come from Great Britain. The trade is largely directed towards the United Kingdom, 54 per cent. of the imports and 26 per cent. of the total trade in 1917–18 being with that country. Even assuming the continuance of the present system, there is always danger in depending too exclusively on a single market.

Shipping is practically all British. The indigenous shipping has entirely disappeared. During the War, Indian trade suffered enormous losses for lack of indigenous shipping.

The exchange banks in India are all foreign. There is a great unsatisfied demand for branch banks and associated banks in the interior. The middlemen derive greater benefits than the producer from the export of local products, because the trade organization of the country is not adapted to the producer's needs. The Government has no organization such as exists in Canada, to enable the producer to obtain the best value in foreign markets for his produce. Official reports exaggerate the value to the country of its foreign trade, since they make no distinction between the trade carried on by the indigenous population, the profits of which are retained in India, and that by the British and foreign agencies.

The people have long been convinced that without political power and Government support, adequate progress is impossible. Substantial transfer of the control over the economic policy of the country into Indian hands is inevitable if conditions are to be improved.

The present gold exchange system under which both the British sovereign and the "token" rupee in India are unlimited tender is by no means satisfactory since it is not "automatic," but has to be "managed." What is required is an effective gold standard. The Indian public should be protected against the losses which result from sharp fluctuations in exchange causing disturbances in the business of the country. The present system has not shown itself satisfactory in this respect during the War; and it further entails—

(1) Coinage of an unnecessarily expensive and yet a "token" coin, viz. the rupee, and

(2) the maintenance of a sterling reserve in London which may be required once in ten or twenty years, and then but partially.

A gold standard would remedy both these evils. If a full-weight and full-value standard gold coin is minted, the exchange may be left to take care of itself. If the currency is placed on a gold basis, as it normally is in Great Britain and every other economically advanced country, the exchange may be safely left to adjust itself as between any two countries.

An effective gold standard does not necessarily imply the excessive circulation of gold coins. In Canada and the United States the currency is gold, but gold dollars are seldom seen, gold notes and gold certificates being commonly used. In a country with a favourable trade balance in normal years, and with very large gold accumulations which an enlightened Government would seek to utilize, there is no question that the technical conditions are present for a successful gold currency. A central State bank or a federal reserve banking system, if established, should maintain the necessary reserve against the issue of currency notes.

These measures would result in the gradual transfer of the paper currency and gold standard reserves amounting to over £90,000,000 (on March 31, 1919) from England to India. This amount, if held in India, would mean so much increase of credit, which would automatically help Indian trade.

The large silver purchases made from time to time may hereafter be negotiated in India instead of in England. With the adoption of an effective gold standard, there will be no need to keep the "token" rupee, 11-12ths fine any more than the four-anna piece.

A proposal for establishing an Imperial Bank for India by amalgamating the existing presidency banks is at present being considered by the Government of India. Amalgamation on the lines proposed would, however, be very undesirable. The present presidency banks may be left to do the banking work of the provinces in which they are situated; and other provinces at present without such banks may be assisted to start new provincial private banks under special arrangements with their Governments.

It would probably be safer for a large country like India to adopt the federal reserve banking system of the United

States rather than the State bank system of France, Germany or Japan. In case the Imperial bank proposal is adopted, the Commonwealth Bank of Australia might serve as a satisfactory model.

The idea of the federal reserve system is to avoid over-centralization of the money power of the country. With all the advantages of a central bank, it possesses also that of decentralized operation, which is helpful to the normal development of the banking facilities of all parts of the country. The local banks are liable to become merely agents of the central bank, and like some of the large deposit banks in France, they may not find it to their interest to promote local industries and commerce.

The foreign-controlled presidency banks in India are patronized by Government, and apathy on the part of Government has very often led to the breakdown of indigenous banking concerns. Under a federal reserve system, this danger would be minimized.

In future, the presidency banks, old and

new, should not be prevented from taking part in foreign exchange work.

For the foreign trade of the country, there should be established a separate exchange bank similar to the Yokohama Specie Bank of Japan. The present exchange banks do not do for the Indian trader what an Indian exchange bank or banks should do, owing to the foreign ownership and European preferences shown by the existing banks. Branches of Indian banks should be established in London, Japan, New York and half a dozen other centres. Canada has several such branch banks in London itself, at present.

There is room for a dozen large private credit banks in India, each with a paid-up capital of fifty lakhs or more. Capital for the purpose should be readily forthcoming.

There should be cross connections between the State bank or banks, the industrial banks mentioned below, and the several credit banks, the latter acting as Government agents in all cases where no federal or provincial bank exists. It is necessary to encourage the formation of banks with large capital by granting for a short period at the commencement such Government help in the way of free audit, guarantee of dividends, etc., as may be required.

An industrial bank should be established in each province, specially adapted to help industries, with power to issue bonds up to ten times the capital subscribed, as in Japan. The Tata Industrial Bank of Bombay, though not exactly of this character, is a beginning in this direction.

The establishment of branch banks should be specially stimulated.

The question of starting an agricultural bank in each province chiefly to finance the co-operative credit societies is also an urgent matter. If cross connections are maintained between all classes of these banks, the securing of which is naturally a function of a State bank or banking system, and if proper checks are maintained, a sound, comprehensive banking system suited to the needs of the country will be permanently established.

Indian trade is further handicapped by the country's abject dependence upon foreign shipping. This subject is separately discussed under the head of Communications in Chapter XI.

In India the movement of goods is completely dependent upon the currents of foreign trade, the internal trade merely registering the movement of raw materials one way and of manufactures the other. But the character of this trade will be different when local industries develop and also when all the usual local businesses like banks or branch banks, hotels, dairies, laundries and transport agencies have been established.

In future, as in the case of Japan, the development of industries and trade, as of production in the districts and sub-districts, should be promoted by the revenue officers of the district with the aid of the necessary technical assistants and staff. To help them there should be semi-official advisory committees for each district and also for each sub-district.

For inter-provincial trade, each province

should maintain trade consuls at the more important cities and ports of other provinces, under the control of the provincial Boards, to be presently referred to. These provincial Boards should have a voice in the regulation of railway tariffs, in order to promote internal trade.

Once the Government is favourable—and no Government which has the interests of the people at heart can be otherwise—it will be easy to bring into existence all the necessary organizations in the way of Government staff and agencies, and other public commercial and industrial institutions and associations. It has already been suggested that a commission with an Indian majority be appointed for a period of five years, to introduce fiscal autonomy and to transform the finances of India from their present form, suited to a dependency, to a form suitable for a self-governing dominion. This will have to be done after careful inquiry into and study of practices gradually introduced into a self-governing dominion like Canada. A central advisory council for commerce and industry and an executive board of commerce and industry, appointed with the consent of the advisory council, should be created to aid the member of council in charge of the department at the Central Government as well as the Minister in each province. Both these bodies should have an Indian majority.

The Board may consist of business men and economic experts, not more than three in number, appointed at the commencement for one year only, but later on for two or three years, at least one fresh nomination being made every year. The officials on the advisory councils should not be allowed to vote. The council should be permitted to advise in matters connected with tariffs. Indian trade commissioners should be appointed in five or six principal foreign countries with which India has large trade relations, in addition to the officer appointed in London. The officer working in London is naturally concerned in finding a market in Britain for Indian food-stuffs and raw materials, but his duties should have a wider scope, and be helpful to Indian merchants and manufacturers. The information collected by the trade commissioners and others should be issued to the public by the Board. Extensive propaganda should be undertaken by Government officers and also by private organizations under the direction of the national and provincial advisory councils referred to.

A journal should be maintained by the Board of Commerce and Industry of each province to publish the information collected by the trade commissioners abroad, provincial trade consuls, travelling deputations and other individuals and bodies, for the information and benefit of the people of the province.

The Board should codify trade practices in civilized countries in a form easily intelligible to local business men. Steps should be taken to introduce a uniform system of weights and measures.

A Chamber of Commerce representing indigenous trade and industry should be established in every province where none exists at present, in addition to an Associated Chamber for all India. Every large city should have a Chamber of Commerce of its own. Every town should have a branch Chamber or a separate commercial association, an information bureau and a museum of agricultural and industrial products. The museum should exhibit corresponding products from advanced countries beside those of local manufacture, so as to stimulate improvement. Many of these associations, though voluntary, may, as in Japan, be incorporated under the law.

The Board should arrange to send, with the aid of Government subsidies, at least half a dozen business men every six months to foreign countries to study trade and industry, and to transact business on their own account.

The promotion of large joint stock companies and the establishment of small concerns for industry and trade, as explained, should form one of the principal duties of the Board. Local men of proved organizing and directing ability should be given every facility and encouragement to start large local enterprises on the joint stock principle. The number of such companies started should be a test of the Board's own efficiency and success.

The principal difficulty in trade, as in every important national activity in which there is international competition, and in which success is dependent on internal co-operation on a large scale, is to get a proper start. In order that this may be done, conditions favourable to the growth of indigenous trade should be created and maintained for fifteen or twenty years, until the people are able to get along without Government aid. It would then be time to think of free trade and open competition. To ask them to develop trade without protective tariffs or political support, while the trade itself is subjected to the fierce competition of the world, is to deny the people the opportunity of making a beginning at all. Government should declare it as their policy that trade by the people of the country shall be fostered by every means in their power, and that none of the expedients adopted for such purposes in advanced countries, or which have proved useful in the past in other parts of the world, shall be in future neglected. All orders and regulations providing trade facilities for the people should take the form of legal enactments or ordinances, so that they may have the force of law, and there may be no going back on them through change of officials.

The provincial University should make abundant provision for giving instruction in the highest branches of technology and commerce. Some large cities may have independent colleges of their own for the purpose. Every district should have high schools giving instruction in technology and in commerce, to form nurseries for training future merchants and business men.

CHAPTER IX

INDUSTRIES

THE industries of a country reflect the productive capacity and executive ability of its inhabitants, and form one of the chief tests of a nation's efficiency. If a pump or an engine were manufactured in India, the people of the country would get exactly the machine they need, and would retain the money which would otherwise go out of the country.

A purely agricultural country which maintains itself by producing only raw material or grain will always remain poor. Under present conditions in India, agriculture gives a bare living, sometimes less than a living, to those who pursue that calling. Without industry and trade in addition, however, it is impossible for India or any country to keep money in circulation or credit easy, and to maintain even an average level of prosperity. Industrial activity is everywhere regarded as a higher species of employment, and is decidedly more remunerative than agriculture.

Some idea may be formed of the position of the larger industries and business concerns in India from the paid-up capital of its joint stock companies, as compared with that of similar companies in more advanced countries.

The capital invested in industrial and commercial concerns in the United Kingdom in 1914 was £2,737,000,000; in Canada, £390,000,000; in the United States of America, £4,558,000,000; and in Japan, £243,000,000. The capital of all the joint stock companies registered in India and held mainly by Indians did not exceed £60,000,000. The total capital of all joint stock companies operating in India was £471,000,000, the greater portion of it, namely, £411,000,000, being of companies registered in England, and presumably held by the people of the British Isles.

When it is remembered that Japan has about one-fifth and Canada less than one-thirtieth of the population of British India, the figures here given are a striking illustration of the low position which India occupies in the industrial world.

While in all the four countries named, much importance is attached to industries, Indians are often told that they must depend chiefly upon the soil for their livelihood. This statement is belied by the practices of the civilized world and the disastrous experience of India herself. Indian manufactures were at one time greatly prized in European and other foreign markets. The old methods of manufacture and credit have, however, become out of date and have gradually fallen into disuse, and, for lack of a policy of development, have not been replaced by new methods, except in a few centres in contact with the foreign population.

At present, raw materials are exported to more enterprising foreign countries and returned to India, or exported elsewhere, in the shape of manufactured articles.

For example, Japan partly uses Indian cotton and exports cotton goods to India and China; Italy does likewise, and exports cotton goods to Turkey in Asia. The people thus suffer a double injury by the export of raw materials fit for local manufacture.

Indians have lost their old industries which, though crude, gave employment to tens of millions of persons. They have to pay for foreign products from their scant earnings from agriculture and other primitive occupations to which a great majority of them are driven by necessity.

This drain from the country is preventable. With a little special effort and co-operation between the Government and the people, it should be easy to supply nearly all the clothing and all the hardware and footwear and other articles needed locally, from India's own factories and looms.

Broadly speaking, the industries of the country may be divided into three classes, namely, (1) large-scale; (2) medium-scale, and (3) minor.

Industries which produce large quantities of products by the employment of considerable capital and labour fall into the first category. They usually require co-operation on a large scale, and a high order of technical skill and organizing ability.

The principal large-scale industries which may be started, or, where they are already started, extended with great advantage to the economic interests of India, are :—

Textiles—cotton, woollen and silk ;

Smelting of ores—manganese, lead, copper, etc. ;

Iron and steel ;

Manufacture of machinery and other articles of iron and steel ;

Shipbuilding ;

Chemical industries—dyes, sulphuric acid, soda ash, artificial manures, etc. ;

Porcelain, glass, cement ;

Paper-pulp and paper ;

Leather industries ; and

Sugar.

In countries like Canada, Japan or Germany, such industries were established either by Government initiative or by active Government encouragement and support. In India, on account of keen foreign competition, such active Government encouragement will, in the beginning, be indispensable. The Government, for one thing, might attempt to manufacture its own stores, if they are not available in India, instead of importing from abroad.

The large-scale industries are best carried on by joint-stock companies, employing a capital of, say, Rs. 15 lakhs or more each.

The minor industries comprise home and cottage industries in cities and towns, and rural or subsidiary agricultural and other industries in towns and villages. They are carried on by individuals or groups of families in a variety of ways as regards provision of raw materials, capital and labour. It may be assumed that the capital employed may be anything up to Rs. 50,000 in each case. The products comprise almost every description of article needed in the country for which raw materials are available. They are manufactured by various methods, in some cases the type of organization being industrial, in other cases, the work being carried on as a domestic employment.

Between the large-scale industries employing a capital of Rs. 15 lakhs or more, and the minor industries working on sums not usually exceeding Rs. 50,000, come a large variety of what may be termed medium-scale industries. These may be owned by individual proprietors, by partnership or by joint stock companies. Some of the products usually manufactured in "large-scale industries" may also be produced by establishments of medium-scale size. The cost of production in such a case will, however, generally be greater.

The Government of India appointed a Commission in 1916 to examine and report upon the possibilities of industrial development in India. The Report has been before the public for some time. It contains many valuable suggestions, but they deal mostly with cottage and small-scale industries, almost ignoring the large-scale ones.

The Commission's most important recommendation is that the Government should start imperial and provincial departments of industries, which should be staffed with experts, at the commencement brought from outside India. The Report provides for imperial and provincial scientific and technical services and a permanent controlling staff.

The entire scheme, it is to be feared, is conceived on wrong lines. The people require help and backing, not control and direction. In the expansion of industries, there are numerous ways in which Government can help or hinder, and not until an atmosphere of sympathy, a spirit of helpfulness and Indian control are established, will industries make any real headway.

The complaint has been made that the policy of railway management has not been helpful to indigenous industries ; that sometimes factory inspectors insist on costly buildings and equipment at the start, which make industries unprofitable ; and that students trained in foreign countries receive scant encouragement. These and other handicaps to industrial development should be publicly investigated and the causes of complaint removed. Even isolated incidents of this sort are likely to be magnified and to cause mischief. They lead to loss of confidence and dishearten the people.

The following are some of the several ways in which Government in India can render direct help :—

Protection of any newly started industry for a term of six years, or till the industry is firmly established, by imposing tariffs on imported goods.

Inducing Indian, British and foreign firms to start industries, particularly machinery and chemical industries, by levying tariffs on imports, as was done in Japan.

Pioneering large and difficult industries, including the manufacture of railway materials and shipbuilding, and also pioneering key industries.

Granting premiums, subsidies and subventions, or guaranteeing dividends to individuals or indigenous companies who show enterprise in starting a new industry.

Providing the services of experts free, or at special low rates, or granting subsidies for the purpose.

Affording special railway facilities.

Taking an industrial census periodically, as required, and publishing statistics.

In most successful countries, the scientific use of tariffs has been a most powerful factor in building up modern industries.

The Provincial Governments may make a start by pioneering some of the larger industries like shipbuilding, machinery, engines, motor transport, chemicals, paper, etc., and also some of the many key industries needed, with the object of making them a success and subsequently transferring them to the people. There are few technical secrets that are not readily available, or that cannot be secured by the expenditure of money.

For the rapid growth of industries, it is first necessary to create an atmosphere of business confidence and a continuity of policy and operations. The development work should be under the advice and control of the leaders of the people closely interested in the work, and represented by the suggested Advisory Council and Board. Government should definitely announce its policy of support and encouragement of industries, which should be ensured by law, as in Japan.

The principal requirements are organizing ability, labour, expert skill, capital, machinery, raw materials and efficient works management. The raw material is available in abundance. For lack of local use it is being exported to foreign countries. The supply of labour is abundant and although in the past there has been a lack of policy for training it, the necessary training could be given in five to ten years. Machinery can be purchased from the best makers if capital is available. Capital will be readily forthcoming if its utilization for the benefit of local industries and enterprise is assured. There will be no necessity to borrow foreign capital at the beginning, although there should be no hesitation in doing so if the rapid growth of industries warrants such a step. Experts should be obtained from wherever they can be secured, and given fees and bonuses, usually in the shape of a moderate monthly salary and payment by results. Some industries may also be advantageously started in co-operation with English and foreign firms.

There will be no dearth of suitable organizers and directors if expert assistance and reasonable financial accommodation are assured. Although college trained men are in charge of the various departments of industries in Japan, the control of the organizations themselves is in the hands of the older class of business men who have shown themselves competent to manage these concerns. If it becomes the settled policy of Government to encourage industrial development, there are many capable merchants and business men of this type among the Indian population who will come forward to take advantage of the opportunities thus afforded. As in Japan, a supply of technical and business graduates should be ensured by starting colleges and institutes without delay. If the industrial development is to succeed the experts and officials employed should be on a temporary tenure and paid by results. The temporary expenditure will be heavy, but rigid official control and resulting stagnation will be avoided.

Reference has been made to the industrial banks needed in the country for financing factory and other large industries. The cash-credit system should be introduced for the benefit of the small industrialist, while co-operative credit is necessary everywhere.

If industrial development is carried on by agreement in spirit and principle between the Government and the people, savings which now are hoarded may be mobilized for financing industries by opening branch banks all over the country. Also by special propaganda, people could be induced to invest, in productive undertakings, much of the unproductive wealth now retained in the shape of jewellery and ornaments in numerous small hoards.

The formation of joint-stock companies for promoting industries requires special encouragement. The law should be examined in the light of the latest developments in foreign countries, particularly in Japan, with a view to adapting it more closely to the local requirements of each province. People will require advice in company flotation. This duty should not be left to company promoters or underwriters. The provincial advisory council of commerce and industry should have the work under its special care for some time, semi-official committees with an expert staff being formed over suitable areas, to advise intending investors and company promoters. The German system under which the banker advises his customer, might also be tried in places. Provincial statistics of the progress of company flotation should be published at least once a month, so that every one interested might watch progress and assist in removing obstacles and providing the necessary help.

Research institutes should be established on the model of the one at Teddington in

England, or the Bureau of Standards at Washington. One such institute will be needed for each province to work in close association with the University and higher technical schools.

Industrial experimental stations like those in Japan, intended for carrying out experiments in manufactures, should be established in every important city and smaller ones in each district, to work in conjunction with the research institutes. These should be maintained at the expense of the State, but should be kept under the administrative control of committees of local business men and experts. Their primary object will be to stimulate experiments and improvements in methods of manufacture, including the testing of processes followed in the various countries. There can be no doubt that such industrial experimental stations are destined to play a great part in India's regeneration.

Industrial museums should be located in every important city, and business inquiry offices in every city and town, to keep in close touch with the experimental stations, research institutes, etc., and obtain up-to-date information and advice for local business men engaged in industries and manufactures.

There should be at least one technical college in each province to teach experimental sciences and industrial chemistry up to the highest standards. Higher technical schools should be established at the head-quarters of each district. Experimental workshops and school laboratories should be associated with them. Short industrial courses should be available for the population of the smaller towns and villages whenever they have leisure to profit by them, particularly in the more extended use of mechanical appliances and machinery.

Had such experimental stations and educational institutions been started in India thirty years ago, she would have made as great an industrial advance as Japan, or perhaps even greater, in view of the enormous resources of both men and raw materials at her disposal.

Correct statistics of industries in every

district and province should be collected and published for the use of the people of the area. They should give all the information and data supplied by industrially advanced countries and they should show clearly the precise share of the indigenous population in every class of enterprise. The coming census should be fully utilized for this purpose. Both Government and public organizations should collect and make available to the people information from foreign countries likely to be of value for developing local industries. The industrial progress of each district, province, city, town and village should be reviewed by the local authorities concerned at least once every year.

There is no doubt that India's productive power can be enormously increased by industries. With money, determination and popular control in a centralized form, and Government help of the character given in Japan, practically any large industry for which raw materials are available can be successfully started in India at the present time.

The present opportunity is extremely favourable for starting industries. As time goes on, competition will grow keener and conditions will become less favourable. To make a satisfactory start, a special effort will be necessary. Large beginnings are not made by routine methods. Government has to raise a loan to establish the necessary research and educational institutions, and also to advance loans, on special terms, to industrial and other banks, to finance industries. The money allotted to each province should be utilized under the direction of the advisory council referred to. The provincial share of the loan may be raised locally in the province concerned, and, if administered in the manner suggested, it will certainly be readily forthcoming.

The work for each province should proceed according to a well-considered programme, approved by the local Legislative Council. The necessary staff should be maintained from the current revenues of the province. It may confidently be expected that the programme will begin to yield definite results in five to ten years from the time work is started. In advanced countries, where every avenue of development is already exploited, returns from new enterprises may be slow, but in a new field like India, and with abundance of cheap labour, industrial activity, when a favourable atmosphere is created, is bound to grow at a rapid pace. The money spent in inaugurating a policy of development will come back to the people and the Government, multiplied a hundredfold.

It is necessary once again to emphasize the statement that this outstanding problem of industry is a matter which concerns the Indian population. If bureaucracy prevails in this department of the country's activity, industries will not prosper. There is no necessity for an Imperial department of industries. A provincial department of industries under Indian control should be maintained. One indispensable duty expected of the Imperial Government is to see that the provincial departments are supplied with funds, that adequate encouragement is given, and that no federal or international restrictions exist to handicap or disable local enterprise. The self-interest of the people and the public spirit of the province will do the rest. As was remarked by a leading London Conservative daily in May, 1920, in referring to the post-war policy of Government in relation to industries in the United Kingdom, "You may have either flourishing industries, or a flourishing bureaucracy, but never both."

CHAPTER X

AGRICULTURE

If all the Indian States are included, as in an economic survey they should be, with British India, the total acreage under cultivation in India is larger than that of any single region of the world, with the possible exception of China and the United States. The estimated value at pre-war rates of the annual production from both dry and irrigated crops may be put down at a little under £400,000,000. This gives an average income of Rs. 33 (£2 4*s.*) per head for the agricultural population, and of about Rs. 24 (£1 12*s.*) per head for the entire population of British India.

Compare the Indian conditions with those of Japan, where agriculture is extremely careful and thorough.

It may be of interest to mention in this

connection that agriculture is carried on in that country very intensively, almost like gardening. Rice seedlings are sown at exact distances apart, measured by a wooden scale. In some of the model villages, the Young Men's Associations carry on experiments themselves, under general advice from the officials.

Japan, although not entirely self-sufficing in the matter of food, maintains normally a population of 56,000,000 on a cultivated area of 17,000,000 acres; that is to say, one-third of an acre per head as against India's five-sixths of an acre. On the normal, pre-war basis, the average production of British India, including irrigated crops, cannot be more than Rs. 25 per acre; in Japan it cannot be less than Rs. 150.

The smallness of the Indian yield is due to a variety of causes, some natural, others avoidable. First comes the rainfall, which, except in Bengal and Burma, is often uncertain. Apart from the relatively small area covered by modern canals, irrigation is restricted to the ancient and arduous method of depending upon tanks and wells. A second cause is the persistence of conservative habits of tillage. Scientific agriculture is almost unheard of, and little practised where known. The *ryot* is extremely simple-minded, and lives in an atmosphere of superstition and tradition. And yet, as many authorities have recognized, he is not altogether disinclined to adopt new ways, provided their value is clearly demonstrated.

The Indian peasant is not essentially different from his fellow in other lands. A little experience would show that he is not lacking in readiness of response—response which would be proportionate to the accessibility and practicable character of the opportunities provided, and to the sincerity and humanity of the people directing the work of instruction and experiment. As agricultural schools and scientific farms are established, continuous effort will have to be made to create a real relationship between the institutions and the agriculturist.

Hitherto, the Indian peasant has been

practically untouched by the feeble and academic attempts at agricultural education, which are all that have been made by the authorities. A few central experimental farms and a number of district farms have been working for several years past; but it cannot be said that they have influenced the general situation in any material degree. They are controlled by Government officials, between whom and the cultivator there is and can be no sympathetic understanding. The policy of agricultural development is controlled, not by experts, but by members of the bureaucracy, who obviously cannot, in the midst of their multitudinous executive duties, keep abreast of the achievements of scientific agriculture in the West. Knowledge, therefore, is lacking, and the technique of modern cultivation is undeveloped. It is no wonder, in these circumstances, that farm operations are conducted for the most part by primitive methods, and that the results, judged by the volume of production, should be distressingly low.

All development being traditionally

associated with bureaucratic initiative and control, capital is shy, and does not flow into agricultural industry ; and it is perfectly plain that until both policy and spirit are radically altered, it will not do so. Local conditions everywhere, coupled with the prevailing ignorance and apathy, make it impossible for bodies of cultivators to combine, as in Russia, Japan, or Western Europe, to promote better farming and better business. The absence of market organization in conjunction with other causes prevents the cultivator from reaping a full reward from his labour. The middleman is also the money-lender, and it is he who profits most. The *ryot*, in consequence, has very little incentive to activity or improvement.

The moral, surely, is obvious. The vast rural problems affecting the welfare of 325,000,000 cannot be handled, cannot even be approached, without special aptitude or training, by a small body of officials encumbered by heavy routine duties, and subject to the rigid habits and prejudices of a hierarchy, embodying, in its clearest form, the principle of imperial ascendancy. The remedy lies in a great and combined progressive movement, including the reform of the official system and the remodelling of Government departments of agriculture. The natural leaders of the people, including prominent agriculturists, should be placed in a position to improve agricultural conditions with the aid of expert assistance, by their own forethought, preparation, and combined effort.

Manifestly, the central aim of all practical measures must be the increase of the yield per acre and the systematic improvement of the product. The most urgent measures needed to lift agriculture from its low level fall under three main heads :—

(1) Provision for the farmer's immediate needs.

(2) Large measures of permanent improvement.

(3) Development of the dynamic forces of rural life.

Under the first head would come such essential necessities as : temporary loans ; facilities for procuring draught cattle, good seed, fertilizers and implements; and instruction in the technique of cultivation and the principles and methods of co-operative effort.

It is desirable at once to establish a large number of seed depots in connection with experimental farms. The supply of chemical manures, especially where irrigation facilities exist, may easily be made highly profitable. Such fertilizers should, as in Canada, be used as far as possible to supplement farm manures, rather than as substitutes for them.

The existing Indian breeds of cattle need improvement, especially for draught purposes. Attention should be given to scientific questions relating to stock breeding and fodder supply.

As to modern implements, while it is true that the Indian farmer needs to be educated in regard to their use, the chief obstacle to progress is the economic inability of the peasant to purchase them. The rapid industrial expansion of India in future, however, will make it easily possible immediately to establish local manufacture on a large scale, so that, given reasonable loan facilities, every cultivator of moderate means might possess or have the use of up-to-date ploughs, pumps and larger agricultural implements, while much might be done to encourage the use of hand-carts and simple labour-saving devices.

Among the larger measures of a permanent character, the first and foremost needed is the establishment of agricultural societies. The success of the individual cultivator now-a-days depends not on himself alone, but on the help and co-operation he may receive from fellow-farmers and leaders, or in other words, on the co-operative effort of the whole locality. Agricultural societies should be established by law, as in Japan, so that the provisions and their execution would not be dependent on the arbitrary will of the officials, but would be binding both on the officials and the rural population.

In Japan, every district, indeed almost every village, has its agricultural society, the scheme, in its national aspect, being a remarkable example of co-ordination. At the head is the Imperial Agricultural Society; below that the prefectural or district society; next the county or city society; and at the base the small town or village society. All are subsidized by Government or local funds. The town and village societies consist wholly of persons actually engaged in agriculture. Altogether, there are some 11,000 such societies in the country.

Associated with the agricultural societies are guilds and other public bodies established by law for the purpose of increasing the quantity and quality of staple products—tea, silk, live stock, etc.—while in various parts of the country private organizations for similar objects are maintained by groups of enthusiastic people. They all share in the common stimulus of a great movement, and at intervals meet in conferences to discuss methods, to compare results, and for the mutual sharpening of minds and purposes.

A few well-managed experimental agricultural farms and schools exist in some of the provinces in India. To bring them into touch with the peasants, they should be under the control of committees composed of experts and the leading representatives of the people engaged or interested in agriculture in the rural areas concerned.

An agricultural farm, assisted by Government funds, should be established in every sub-district and every important village where people desire to have such an institution. These farms, and the laboratories attached to the agricultural colleges, should provide facilities for carrying on specific research work to obtain estimates of yield as a result of the various special methods and appliances utilized. Short courses in economy should be conducted in the experimental farms during the seasons of the year when farming operations are not brisk.

Clearly the main necessity is to gather into the agricultural schools as many people as possible for instruction in the rudiments of scientific agriculture, while the more enterprising farmers should be encouraged to go through the general farmers' course, at the institutes and experimental farms. The curriculum of the schools should comprise such objects as soils, seeds, live stock, home economics, elementary business principles and accountancy, while provision should be made, for the reasons dealt with above, for training in subsidiary occupations. The best way, indeed the only way, by which science can be made to appeal to the rural mind is through the medium of common experience and practical results. Hence, the farmer should be encouraged not only constantly to seek to improve his own knowledge, but to take advantage of opportunities for having his womenfolk instructed in the household crafts.

The cultivator should receive training in husbandry by observing the work on well-managed farms. Instruction in scientific agriculture should be imparted both on the farms and in agricultural schools. The highest form of agricultural education should be imparted in the university, where the specialists, research workers, expert farm managers and leaders capable of formulating an agricultural policy and introducing new and profitable methods of cultivation will be trained. A secondary grade education will be required to equip a class of intermediaries to carry out the plans of the leaders and interpret them to the peasants. A class of agricultural engineers or *maistries* is urgently required to work as lecturers and instructors, to form a link between the experimental stations and the agricultural societies or the actual farmers themselves.

Special institutions, where needed, should also be provided for carrying on experiments in sericulture, in cattle, sheep and horse breeding, and other agricultural pursuits. A staff of inspectors and lecturers should be employed in each district associated with the district farms, to help the agricultural societies and through them, the cultivators, by demonstrations, discourses and propaganda work generally.

During the past half-century, agricultural indebtedness in India has grown markedly through various causes. Among them are the pressure of the people on the land; partitioning and re-partitioning into uneconomic holdings; the Contract Act of 1872, which transformed the old human relations between the money-lender (*sowcar*, *baniya* or *mahajan*) and the *ryot* into the legal relation of debtor and creditor; the date of the land revenue collection which compels the *ryot* to borrow before he can realize his harvest at the best market rates; the use made of the money-lender as dealer by agents of the great foreign firms; absence of a communal market system; the decay of village arts and crafts.

Beyond question, the initial steps towards dealing with the vast problem of rural indebtedness should be the wide extension of co-operative credit, and the gradual transformation of the existing system by the adaptation of methods proved valuable in countries like Russia, Denmark and Ireland. In Government reports of the past decade, the growth of co-operative credit has made a brave show year by year, but all that has so far been done amounts only to a scratching of the surface. The societies now existing fall into four classes: (1) credit, (2) purchase, (3) sale and (4) production. The great majority, however, are credit societies, and these need to be remodelled and greatly expanded before we can hope to see in India anything corresponding with the movement that forms so hopeful a feature of agricultural life in Japan—the effective co-ordination of the various kinds of agricultural societies for the constant vitalizing of the rural community.

A central agricultural bank like the Hypothec Bank of Japan is needed to subsidize co-operative societies and supply the capital required for developing agriculture. The district banks started with local money and enterprise may receive help from the central bank similar to the help afforded by the Japanese Hypothec Bank. A properly co-ordinated network of such banks will help to mobilize all available capital and largely diminish the tendency towards hoarding.

The farmer has much need of subsidiary occupations in India. As the agricultural holdings are small, and the rainfall is limited to four or five months in the year, he is fully employed only for about six months out of twelve. After an unsatisfactory monsoon, large numbers suffer from unemployment, and in times of famine, the entire body of agriculturists go without work. It is a question of life and death to the people that there should be a diversity of occupations in rural areas.

The occupations usually practised are fruit and dairy farming, sericulture, weaving, rearing cattle, pigs and poultry, preparing ghee, vegetables, etc., for the market. Multitudes of artisans employed as carpenters, masons, smiths, barbers, washermen, etc., follow agriculture as a subsidiary profession. There are numerous small and home industries practised in Japan which may be introduced into rural areas in India. In the neighbourhood of forests, forest industries should be encouraged, and near the sea-board and lakes, fishing.

Provision should be made for instructing children in these and other suitable rural industries; capital should be provided by co-operative effort, and by Government loans where necessary. The question of market organization should receive special attention.

The new department of industries might organize a plan of operations, by which the subsidiary industries of an area may be assured of all reasonable co-operation with financial help and encouragement from the local authorities and public associations.

The subject of irrigation will be separately dealt with, in the next chapter, under the head of development of natural resources and communications.

Hitherto, the science of statistics has been, for the cultivator, either a matter altogether outside his range, or another means of vexation devised by Government officials. This ought not to be the case. Agricultural progress is not possible in the modern world without statistics, and it is clear that increasing importance will be attached to the collection and use of facts and figures relating to production, including those of subsidiary occupations. The village group should be taken as a unit, and statistics of the entire province should be so compiled as to be easily intelligible to the ordinary literate cultivator. The results should be made accessible in all localities for study and reference, and comparisons instituted with reference to other provinces and foreign countries. Rightly treated, the collection of facts may itself be a means of communal effort and education.

The statistics should reflect the general condition of the cultivator, the area of his holding, the number of draught and milch cattle in his possession, the amount of capital (tools, implements and other property) possessed by him, the area of his indebtedness, the total production of the farm, his income from subsidiary occupations, the number of working members of the family, etc. A frequent census should be taken of production, so as to include all these particulars.

The usual criticism levelled against the Indian is that he is a creature of the day, or the season; that he lives from hand to mouth. The plain fact is that harsh circumstance forces him to do so. Merely to keep alive is a problem for him. He cannot give thought to the necessity of preparing in advance for probable bad seasons. Long ago, no doubt, under the ancient village constitution, a year's sustenance could be stored against famine; but the growth of the modern system of administration has made such expedients impossible. To-day, agricultural India suffers from overpowering inertia. Before a new order can be introduced into the villages, the spirit of hope and enterprise must replace the prevalent apathy and despair.

The first practical step is to enable Indians in increasing numbers to see for themselves what science is doing to improve agriculture throughout the world. Parties of representative men, from every province, should be encouraged to travel abroad, especially to Japan. These parties should include not only men of wealth and high position, but also, as a matter of course, teachers, farmers, members of the provincial services, and graduates of agricultural colleges. The information and specimens brought back by them should be made use of for local exhibitions, and they should be required to disseminate knowledge acquired by them while travelling abroad, through every available channel.

It must, however, be emphasized that nothing can be done until the local administration becomes thoroughly imbued with a new spirit. Every opportunity must be given to people of village, *taluk*, or district, to co-operate with one another to carry out works of public improvement, such as making and repairing roads and bridges, constructing irrigation tanks and channels, improving sanitation and the like. The present conditions of local administration make it impossible for the cultivators to co-operate in the performance of such needful services. The people, cut off as they are from responsibility and self-help, are, to all intents and purposes, dead. The only thing that can save the Indian body politic from dissolution is the transfusion of new life into the system of governance by the gradual devolution of authority. India has abundant resources in the shape of capital, labour and natural directive talent, but at present they are locked up.

District farm bureaux have been started and turned to admirable use in various Western countries during recent years. In the United States, for example, over a million farmers are organized through such bureaux, and are thereby enabled to grapple co-operatively with local problems. In some States, wherever one-fifth of the farmers in a county wish for a farm bureau, the administration provides an adviser and staff, and makes an annual grant. A close connection exists between the farm bureaux and the agricultural colleges, now flourishing in every State. By such means constant intercourse and stimulus are provided for the whole agricultural community.

In India, the first necessity is to create an atmosphere of confidence and co-operation. That done, there can be no doubt of the growth of a movement of multiple improvement, which, we may assume, would express itself in common effort for insurance against famine. Each family will be able to lay by a little store of grain; co-operative granaries will spring up; the wasteful use of cow-dung as fuel will be checked; plantations for the supply of fuel will be started; labour-saving appliances will come into use, and subsidiary occupations will multiply. The cultivator will rapidly become conscious of the progress that is being effected. He will provide himself with footwear, and with a more adequate protection from the tropical sun than the piece of cotton cloth in which his head is now wrapped. He will eat his food not from leaves or earthen vessels, but from plates of porcelain, brass, or copper. As the results of modern knowledge are gradually unfolded before him, he will realize that the bonds of necessity are breaking, and that he need no longer go on with his hopeless daily labour, content, like his ancestors, to scratch the surface of the earth merely to keep life in his body.

The Government should have programmes for increasing production and agricultural development generally prepared for every district and sub-district, and should maintain statistics of production, review progress, and issue an annual report for the district, showing to what extent the cultivators have been helped by the institutions and organizations created for their benefit, and with what result.

While agriculture cannot bring wealth to India on a great scale, if the measures here sketched be taken up, the production of the country might, on a moderate estimate, be doubled within fifteen years or even less. The extension of cultivation, increased irrigation, rotation of crops, intensive cultivation with the fullest use of fertilizers, and improvement in stock-breeding are all urgently needed. The most speedy way of promoting these ends is to give leadership and financial support to the agriculturist, while all the while encouraging him to feel that he is the master of his own business, and that the officials connected with agricultural instruction and administration are there merely to counsel and assist him. When, in the years to come, the Indian people travel more freely, when both general and special education comes to be more widely spread, the idea of conscious and systematic development will take firm root in the country.

On this subject one more observation remains. The suggestion of village unions or grouping of villages already recommended in the chapter on Local Self-Government, if immediately adopted, will introduce order and a spirit of development into rural areas, and will, we may confidently expect, be the speediest means of rehabilitating the communal life of the Indian countryside.

CHAPTER XI

DEVELOPMENT OF RESOURCES AND COMMUNICATIONS

IRRIGATION works are of vital importance in a tropical country like India, where there are tracts in which not a blade of grass can grow on unirrigated soil. The total irrigated area of British India is about 48,000,000 acres, or 21 per cent. of the total net cropped area of 230,000,000 acres, of which 26,000,000 are watered by canals built by the State, and the remaining 22,000,000 by tanks and wells constructed by private agency. About 6,000,000 acres of land in the Indian States are also irrigated.

The total outlay on the State irrigation works for which capital accounts are kept, amounts to Rs. 730,000,000, and the value of crops raised on such areas to Rs. 970,000,000. The larger works, classed as productive, gave a return of 8·1 per cent. in 1918–19. Thus, for every Rs. 100 spent on capital irrigation works, the country obtains, making allowance for temporary high prices, a gross produce of Rs. 100 or more annually, a fact which should commend this class of works to public favour.

The irrigation policy at present followed in India is based upon the recommendations of an Indian Irrigation Commission, which sat between 1901–03, during Lord Curzon's Viceroyalty. That Commission estimated that $12\frac{1}{2}$ per cent. of the total rainfall was utilized in artificial irrigation of all kinds in India. The annual surface flow of the river basins of India, excluding Burma, Assam and Eastern Bengal, amounted, according to the Commission, to 51,000,000 cubic feet, of which only 6,750,000 cubic feet were actually utilized in irrigation. The balance passed to waste in the sea. Reservoirs, tanks and canals must be constructed to utilize some of this waste water with profit to the people and to the State.

In future annual reports the permanent

policy and plans in respect of each province should be briefly stated, and forecasts of projected irrigation works published for the information of the public.

The rapid development of industries and transportation, and the supply of power and light for cities and towns, largely depends upon cheap fuel. Of the 120,000,000 horse-power used in the various countries of the world for all purposes—railways, factories, shipping, etc.—75,000,000 horse-power is used in factories and for municipal activities, 13,000,000 horse-power being thus used in the United Kingdom alone. Canada has already developed roughly 2,300,000 horse-power from her water-power resources, which potentially amount to nearly 20,000,000 horse-power.

Under the orders of the Government of India, the "white-coal" or water-power resources of the Indian continent were recently surveyed. The preliminary report which has been issued gives some details.

At a rough estimate, the total power supplied in India is put down at less than

1,200,000 horse-power. Of this, 285,000 is electric horse-power, of which only 36 per cent. is obtained from water-power. As all the rainfall is precipitated in four or five months of the year, storage reservoirs are necessary to obtain a continuous flow for power generation throughout the year.

The Cauvery Power Works in Mysore and the Tata scheme in Bombay are the pioneer hydro-electric works in India. Both are undergoing development. In future the Government and the people should actively interest themselves and co-operate in developing this branch of power supply, for which there is a growing demand.

Though the total forest area of British India is nearly 250,000 square miles, the total net revenue derived from forest products was only a little over £1,000,000 in 1918–19. The public has little information about the work of this department. It is, therefore, impossible to make a dogmatic statement in regard to India's potentialities in this respect. There can be no doubt, however, that better commercial use can be made of the forests with a view to providing materials for industries and increasing the revenue.

The Indian forests are, at present, utilized to a small extent to supply timber for building purposes, fuel for domestic use, wood for paper-pulp, and minor produce of various kinds. It has yet to be officially recognized that a forest is a crop, and not a mine which can be left undeveloped indefinitely, and that wood will rot unless cut and removed at the proper intervals.

Land should be given, on favourable terms, for private plantations, with a view to encouraging the people to grow trees of economic value. Permanent plots should be established to experiment with pulp woods. Companies for the manufacture of paper, where necessary in co-operation with British manufacturers, should be started in the vicinity of large forests. As in Canada, Government should endeavour to build up forest industries and establish more forest schools.

Local provincial and district committees should be associated with the officials in charge of the forests, so that the people may closely follow the work that is being done, and assist in building up this important State property. Such committees should also draw public attention to the possibilities of particular forest industries such as paper, matches, pencils, furniture, etc. Reliable estimates of the value of forest products in each area should be maintained from year to year, and published periodically for the information of the local population.

The old mining and mineral industries have died out in India, and the people of the soil are very inadequately associated with the modern mining industries started in the country. According to the *Indian Year Book* for 1919, the modern developments in Europe have "helped to stamp out in all but remote localities, the once flourishing manufactures of alum, the various alkaline compounds, blue vitriol, copperas, copper, lead, steel and iron, and seriously curtailed the export trade in nitre and borax."

The gross value of mineral production in

1917 was £13,500,000—exceedingly small for so large a country as India, and possessed of such vast resources. The corresponding production in Canada in the year 1917 was £40,000,000; in Japan, £44,000,000; and in the United States of America, £430,000,000.

The principal minerals produced in India in 1917 were coal to the value of £4,500,000; gold, £2,300,000; manganese ore, £1,500,000; petroleum, £1,100,000; and salt, £900,000. Most of these industries are in non-Indian hands.

Neither the Government nor the leaders have made any attempt to prepare the public to engage in mining work. The information relating to geological surveys is not published in a form that is intelligible to the lay public or calculated to stimulate indigenous enterprise in mining.

India's mines should be nationalized as regards ownership, though they may be worked by companies, or individuals. Each provincial Government should be free to deal with the local minerals in the interests of the people of that province.

It may be mentioned that the Japanese

Government at first undertook to work some of the principal mines in Japan as models, employing foreign mining engineers and geological experts for the purpose. The mines were, however, transferred to private ownership as soon as they began to be successful.

Colleges and Schools of Mining and Metallurgy are needed for training alike in the highest scientific branches and in practical work. At least two colleges giving the highest instruction obtainable should be started at once. Also a number of schools in the existing mining centres. There should be a recognized co-ordinated scheme of such instruction for all India.

An advisory committee should be associated with the bureau or department of mines in each province. As in Canada, under similar circumstances, the Central Government may confine its attention to scientific investigations and to the collection of information from foreign countries for dissemination among the people. Pamphlets embodying reliable information regarding local resources, together with advice and instruction for exploitation, both in English and in the vernacular, should be issued by the provincial geological departments from time to time. The question should be considered whether the provincial Governments should not undertake the establishment of smelting furnaces, rather than let ores be exported in their crude state. Canada is doing this as regards copper, and Australia as regards spelter.

India's natural resources have never been thoroughly surveyed. It is, therefore, difficult to estimate her potentiality. A special commission should be appointed to undertake this task.

Among industrial possibilities to be surveyed may be mentioned the manufacture of salt, the development of fisheries, the preservation of game, etc. There is no reason why all the salt needed should not be manufactured in the country itself.

Fisheries at one time received some attention in Madras, but no large measures have been put into operation and no schools established with a view to increasing from that source the food supply of the population.

On account of high mountain barriers on the north, north-west and north-east, India, so far as foreign communications are concerned, is practically an island. Civilized life cannot be maintained without more intimate association with foreign lands. The total tonnage of shipping entered and cleared in India amounted to 17,000,000 tons in 1913–14, and less than 11,000,000 tons in 1917–18. In Canada the total tonnage entered and cleared in 1917–18 was 29,000,000 tons. In the single port of Detroit, situated upon the shore of an inland lake in the United States which is ice-bound for four or five months in the year, the tonnage entered and cleared amounted to over 100,000,000 tons in 1916. Considering that India has a coast-line 4,500 miles long, her shipping facilities are utterly inadequate for the trade of the country. There are only six or seven developed harbours in the whole country. The shipping is, moreover, all foreign.

Even foreign-built ships "registered" in India form a paltry one or two per cent. of the total tonnage employed in the foreign and coastwise trade of the country. Indian construction is required as well as Indian registration.

In the middle of the last century there were 34,000 Indian-owned vessels with an aggregate tonnage of 1,250,000. Towards 1900, these had dwindled to a tonnage of a little over 100,000. During the War, a few small vessels were constructed, presumably for use in Mesopotamia, but it is safe to say that for all practical purposes there is to-day no Indian-owned shipping.

It is necessary in the interests of the country for the Government in India to start building ships on its own account. It should be able to build ships in its own yard for the Royal Indian Marine. Even if nothing more could be done than to assemble parts in India, the industry would give profitable employment to a large number of people.

Australia has purchased all private ships, started shipbuilding yards, and nationalized the whole industry, including the working.

In Japan the State took the initiative in shipbuilding and iron and steel manufacture, although raw materials for these two industries were not so easily procurable in Japan as they are in India.

In Canada and the United States, as already stated, shipbuilding is going on at a rapid rate under Government auspices. At present, both America and Japan are trying to carry on all their trade with India in their own bottoms, as the Germans and Austrians tried hard to do in pre-war years.

The provincial Governments should, according to circumstances, be able to spend specific sums of money every year on the construction and development of ports. District and city Boards should also take part and be given an interest in the financial results of port development schemes.

The railway mileage open for traffic in India in 1917–18 amounted to 36,000 miles, of which one-half was broad gauge (5 ft. 6 in.). The average return on the capital expenditure (about £365,000,000) on railways in that year amounted to about seven per cent.

The Railway Act, especially in its administration, is at present extremely unsatisfactory. The provisions for the protection of life and property need to be strengthened. The liability of railways to compensate the public for material and pecuniary injuries needs to be increased. There have been numerous protests against the owner's risk notes under which railways charge the full freight rate without assuming liabilities. No civilized country permits carriers to do this. The entire policy of fixing rates should be revised so that railways will not appear to exist primarily to assist the export trade, largely in non-Indian hands, rather than to increase the prosperity of the indigenous population.

The railways may be said to be already mostly nationalized so far as ownership is concerned. If, in future, the working of the railways were undertaken by Government agencies instead of being entrusted to private companies, public revenues would be greater, since profits would not have to be shared with the companies as is the case at present.

The railway workshops should be utilized more largely and without racial distinction for the training of local foremen and mechanics. More than half of the railway Board should, in future, be composed of Indian business men. Food and other conveniences should be provided for the poorer classes of the travelling public under stipulated standard rules. All railway stores should either be manufactured in State factories or purchased in India.

The use of motor-cars and motor transport has developed only within the past twenty-five years. Development in this respect has, however, been exceedingly rapid in the United States of America, where motor-cars are manufactured by the million and where an abundant supply of cheap gasoline is available. In the Western States of America horse conveyances have practically disappeared. Most farmers use motor-cars. There is said to be an average of one car for every eight persons in that part of the country. At the beginning of 1920 there were 7,600,000 motor-cars in use in the United States, whereas the total number in use in the whole of Europe did not exceed 500,000. The figures for India are not available, but they must be comparatively very small.

If the Government were to do no more than to give their goodwill, and if the import duty on petroleum were regulated with the consent of the leading Indian business men, a great motor-car industry could be established in India within a year. There are firms ready to start if only they could be assured of Government co-operation and support.

It is probable that within the next decade air transport will be the most powerful factor in the development of every country commercially, economically and socially. Schools should be immediately started to train Indians in civil aerial transport. India should not lag behind other countries either in the construction or navigation of aircraft.

Traffic and commerce cannot be extended without good roads and cheap means of transportation.

Roughly 200,000 miles of roads, of which 55,000 were metalled and 145,000 were unmetalled, were maintained by the public authorities in India in 1916–17. In 1917–18, Rs. 5,000,000 were spent upon military, Rs. 600,000 upon civil Imperial, and Rs. 5,200,000 on civil provincial roads, making a total expenditure upon roads of Rs. 10,800,000.

All roads other than Imperial or provincial should be maintained by local bodies, with the general advice and financial and technical help of the provincial Board. Before new roads are constructed, provision should be made for their upkeep. Cart tracks from village to village should be left to the villagers themselves. Field tracks for conveying produce, especially in irrigated areas, are insufficient in many parts of the country and should be immediately augmented. With a little advice and persuasion, the people will be quite willing to find both the money and labour for this purpose.

The time will soon come, if it has not already arrived, when the bullock cart will be found altogether too slow. Good roads are, therefore, becoming increasingly important. Light four-wheeled carts should take the place of two-wheeled carts. Small handcarts or barrows would save the rural population the labour involved in carrying head loads. Such carts would only require narrow tracks, as in Japan.

Numerous streams are unbridged. A bridge construction programme should, therefore, be formulated for each district and some progress made from year to year, with the aid of contributions from the provincial Government.

There is not much scope for inland navigation in India except on the river and canal systems of Eastern Bengal, Burma and Sindh, and, in a small way, in Madras. The public require precise information as regards existing facilities and the scope for improvement.

Such inland navigation as is possible has been reduced by manipulation of railway rates so as to make it uneconomic. Coasting trade viâ Broach to Bombay was crushed in this way, as was also transport by water between Allahabad and Calcutta. Methods of this sort are doubly damaging to industries, for they cause congestion on railways and destroy indigenous enterprise, which largely controls inland navigation.

On account of the large volume of business centred in cities, traffic becomes congested unless communications are improved from time to time. Hard surface roads with suitable footpaths, underground and overhead railways, surface tramways, motor and animal draught conveyances are needed in some of the larger cities. The cities of Bombay and Calcutta require underground railways. It is understood that a tube railway project for Calcutta is under consideration. Suburban railways are needed in many cities to enable the business population to reside in healthy localities near their work. These conveniences will, however, be too costly, and the actual construction will be too slow, unless the necessary iron and steel are manufactured locally.

More and better postal, telegraph and telephone facilities are needed in India.

Private individuals and companies should be allowed to construct and work telephones with a licence from the local authorities.

When all is said and considered, the greatest resource of the country and the one hitherto least utilized is the energy and intelligence of its people. A way must be found largely to associate Indians with the work of developing the country's resources.

For a generation or more to come, development may best be undertaken by bringing into existence, with legal sanction, local corporations in each region or area. The business men with organizing and directing ability should be brought together in each area and encouraged to form themselves into corporations for the development of local resources. In any particular district, for instance, there may be mining corporations, irrigation corporations, corporations for developing road and motor traffic where such traffic may be found to be profitable, corporations for developing forest resources, public utilities, and water-power and specific industries which require Government co-operation. In all undertakings which are not carried on by purely private enterprise, the capital and the directing energy should, as far as possible, be derived from the area itself. Graduates from the local areas should be trained to take a leading part in the work. If such training is commenced at once, the supply of local talent will be found, within a period of from five to ten years, quite equal to all the development work in each province and district. The work of the corporations will itself be a good training ground. The country should not, in future, be allowed to suffer for lack of such preparation and training.

The work of development referred to in this chapter may be carried out in three ways: (1) By purely private corporations or agencies; (2) by Government and private agencies working in co-operation; and (3) entirely by Government agencies. The three chief requirements for this work are organizing and directing skill, capital and labour. Organizing and directing agency is nowadays quite as important as capital, and Indians must be trained for such employment. Some of the development work under irrigation, forests, railways, etc., may be carried out by means of loans raised locally. Notwithstanding the criticisms levelled at Indian workers, there is no doubt that, if suitably trained and organized, the supply of both skilled and unskilled labour will be inexhaustible.

Government should appoint a commission of conservation for each province. Each bureau or branch of development work in the province should have a committee of non-officials, experts and officials, associated with its head.

A central commission should co-ordinate the work of these provincial bodies, prepare designs, and suggest new developments.

Only the largest works in each province should be carried out by Government or contractors working under Government supervision. All ordinary schemes, and even costly projects requiring only ordinary skill, should be entrusted to corporations of local contractors and business men.

In this manner, many works may be

built and assets created in the provinces with local capital, enterprise and labour. This will be the most natural and healthy form of development, both as regards equipping the people with skill, and creating public property in each region.

Social Reconstruction

CHAPTER XII

BETTERMENT OF SOCIAL CONDITIONS

EVERY care should be taken by the Government and people alike so to direct the work of reconstruction that, in industrializing India, the fullest possible advantage is taken of Western and Japanese experience to avoid creating labour complications, evil housing conditions and such other grave urban problems.

In the chapter on Local Self-Government, reference has already been made to certain needs of urban progress and of rural development. A few additional notes on the same subject may not be out of place in their relation to social betterment.

The smallness of the urban population in India has already been dwelt upon as one of her serious drawbacks. The agricultural character of the population has been maintained, hitherto, by limiting the urban areas and omitting to encourage industries likely to attract people from the country to the cities and towns.

Some Indians may fear that the proposed increase of the urban population will only add to the existing slums and may point to the movement in Western countries which seeks to take the city dwellers "back to the land." These critics must be reminded, however, that many of the Indian villages are hardly better than slums; that if urban reconstruction be undertaken, the increase in urban population need not add blocks of slums to towns, and that many years must elapse before the urban population in India comes anywhere near that of countries where city overcrowding has created a need for people to return to the land. In many cases industries could be developed in or near the new group villages, and thus large urban districts might grow up under healthy and well-planned conditions, with broad streets, open spaces and such-like amenities.

Each city and large town in India, as

already suggested, should have a separate improvement Board under the municipal council to prepare schemes for expanding the areas under its jurisdiction and for the construction of houses on good models.

In cities such as Berlin, extensions are planned and drains are constructed before building operations are begun. Owing, however, to the primitive conditions prevailing and lack of forethought in India, houses are built first, and only when sanitation becomes a crying need are drains thought of! Often streets are only opened after houses have been built.

Parks, playgrounds, theatres, museums, art galleries and other means of public recreation and instruction should exist in every urban area, together with readily accessible railway and tramway facilities, boulevards and other means of transit and communication.

It is of the first importance that sufficient space should be preserved for the natural growth of the locality. The local authority, too, should not fail to recover for itself a considerable portion of the increase in land values arising from public improvements.

As all cities, towns and villages are to have true self-government, it should soon be possible to insist upon a high standard of sanitation and civic utilities. At present, urban areas are allowed to grow up without regulation or organization. Serious attention needs to be given to the question of housing not only the industrial workers, but the people in general. In villages there are few properly built brick or stone houses, and it is quite common to find cattle and human beings living under the same roof.

Houses in towns are more substantial, but even they, as a rule, leave much to be desired. Little attention is paid to the ensuring of sanitary conditions. In order to raise the standard of living, a desire for better housing must be aroused and the people taught to appreciate the advantage of substantial masonry houses with tiled or terraced roofs. Such dwellings promote the health and comfort and therefore the efficiency of the people, whilst overcrowding reduces a nation's efficiency and working capacity, and leads to many other evils.

The local authorities might set a good example by building a decent class of houses for their own servants and for all labourers engaged on public works. At the same time, building societies and companies on co-operative lines should be encouraged. In England, since the War, voluntary societies, commercial firms and local authorities are all carrying on more or less extensive building operations, whilst the Government constantly urges the matter forward and is helping with grants of money.

Every house-owner should see that proper masonry drains and receptacles are constructed so that refuse water may not sink into the soil and form cesspools reeking with contagion. Separate receptacles with tight lids should be provided for dry refuse. It should be the duty of the municipal or other local authorities concerned to remove the contents of these receptacles. The sale of refuse to cultivators can sometimes be made a source of revenue to the local authority.

A great waste of human labour is involved in the management of households, particularly in old-fashioned methods of cleaning and cooking, based on tradition rather than on the scientific requirements of cleanliness, order and finish. In these days of labour-saving and time-saving appliances, domestic economy has become a fine art, and it should not be necessary for women to spend so large an amount of time in domestic work as they do now.

With suitable appliances and arrangements, even the ordinary non-domestic man can prepare, cook, serve and consume a meal, and wash up and put by the utensils, all in the space of little more than an hour; whereas in India the women of the household make several hours' work of cooking even for a small family. Instruction in domestic economy and art should be provided in schools and special institutions in every city or town ward and in at least every central village.

To promote the social and cultural life of the people, every local authority must bring into existence clubs, reading-rooms, libraries, associations, etc., upon the model of those in progressive countries. Meeting places for people to come together, think together, and work together are indispensable for that co-operative effort which should be the watchword of the future.

If business enterprise is to be developed there must be a sufficiency of accommodation for travellers. In large cities there are hotels and satisfactory food supplies for foreign travellers, but no corresponding organization exists for Indians themselves, who when travelling are therefore subjected to many privations. The accommodation available for them either takes the form of caravanserais which do not provide food, making it necessary for them to carry their household goods along with them and do their own cooking; or a poor class of eating-houses where only the roughest meals are served and no lodging arrangements nor ordinary sanitary conveniences exist.

If the local authorities, perhaps with the

assistance of voluntary societies, provide decent and comfortable hostels for travellers and others, they will be able to set a good standard for this class of enterprise which may eventually be taken up by local business men. If managed on modern lines they can be made to pay and also to promote the business interests, comfort and convenience of the people.

One of the first necessities of the country is the provision of abundant travelling facilities by rail and road for the middle and poorer classes of the indigenous population, including proper accommodation for eating and sleeping *en route*. Special care must be taken not to offend against caste rules or to wound susceptibilities. In time, however, it is to be hoped that common dining arrangements on a non-caste basis will become acceptable to the majority of the people, higher rates being charged for caste arrangements.

As a beginning, Government should insist on all railway administrations providing these facilities for the indigenous population, whilst the municipalities or other local authorities should discharge this duty for their own areas. At the outset, some loss may be involved, but it is a public duty which should be fulfilled by the local authority until private enterprise takes it over.

It has already been seen that a low standard of living arises from the fact that agriculture is the one industry and consequently overcrowded. Arts and crafts having decayed and modern industry not having emerged to take their place, there is no organization or co-operation in the business life of the country. The average earning power amounts to about Rs. 180 for a family of five persons. Thirty years ago, the average income of a family in India or Japan was about the same. To-day it is safe to say that the average earning power in Japan is three times what it is in India.

One thing necessary towards raising the standard of life is the cultivation of the saving habit. The agricultural classes particularly are in the habit of contracting debts without any thought of repayment. It should be reckoned a condition of respectability for every useful citizen at all times to have enough savings to carry him through two years of distress or lack of employment.

In advanced countries, people procure protection against unemployment, old age, sickness or accident by systems of insurance, partly through voluntary societies and partly by State or municipal schemes which in Germany, Great Britain and some other countries are compulsory. Under the National Insurance scheme of Great Britain, weekly payments for medical insurance for employees are levied—one proportion from the employee, one proportion from the employer and one proportion from the public funds.

A serious attempt should be made in India by every means possible to reduce poverty and to raise the standard of living. By education and organization it should be possible to abolish poverty altogether. Many people have regarded poverty as a social blessing. In the West, at all events, such ideas are now passing away and poverty is being rightly thought of as a great barrier across the path of civilization—as a social disease which must be cured and prevented.

By the aid of large-scale production and a general system of co-operation, poverty should be made impossible. The model villages of Japan have set an example in this respect which might be profitably followed by their Indian prototypes.

Labour all the world over, it must be remembered, is in revolt against bad treatment, sweating, slum life, and the other unsatisfactory conditions to which modern industry has subjected it. In India, too, the ignorance of the people has been exploited by capitalists and employers, and it is, therefore, not surprising that there should be increasing tension between capital and labour.

It is extremely desirable that India, thus early in her industrial history, should face the problems which in Europe and America have caused so much misery in the past, and are at present the occasion of so much strife and dislocation of business.

Better treatment should be ensured in

future by giving the workers the opportunity of voicing their views in the Legislative Councils, through trade organizations, the Press, etc. ; also by providing economic education which will fit at least the abler among them to appreciate the complexity of the affairs with which they deal and to advance the interests of their class.

After the formation of the German Empire, some of the leading German economists urged upon the Government and the employers the necessity for raising wages and improving labour conditions so that the German working-man might, by increased energy and physique, produce as much as the British working-man, and help to wrest the trade from Great Britain. It was clearly believed in Germany that Great Britain's supremacy towards the end of the last century was due to the superior conditions under which the producers lived.

While employers should improve the wages and living conditions of their employees, the workers on their part might realize their own shortcomings. For instance, they neither work regularly nor organize efficiently. Every possible stimulus should be given both by Government and private endeavour to improve the national working habits so that productive power and earnings may be increased.

Inefficiency may, to a certain extent, be eliminated by the prevention of sickness and degeneracy, as well as by suitable education for the individual. This would not in itself, however, entirely do away with poverty, for so long as a purely competitive and profit-making system continues a portion of the population will remain poor.

The real solution of the problem lies in co-operation. By working together, each for all and all for each, the workers would be able themselves to reap the profits of large-scale production which under any but the co-operative system will go too largely into the pockets of the capitalist. The modern expedients of piece-work payment, profit-sharing, etc., should therefore be discussed by employers and public men alike, with a view to stimulating production and raising wages.

It would be necessary to appoint a commission to examine the trend of the labour movement with a view to avoiding the mistakes which have been made by other nations and solving Indian problems in the light of reason. The commission should be formed chiefly of Indians, with experts and officials added, and must be ready to face two or three years' hard work and study.

From all that has been said it is clear that the country has a great deal to learn from outside experience. Indians will do well to arrange, through central organizations, to send deputations of selected men and women to foreign countries to study all that can be learned of improved methods of civic government and social practices, with a view to adopting the most suitable models.

Civics should form part of the social science courses of every university.

In every primary and secondary school, too, a spirit of citizenship should be aroused among the pupils, and the elements, at least, of civic government imparted to them.

If the highest national ideals are to be fully realized in the future, they must first be created in the minds of youth.

CHAPTER XIII

SOCIAL REFORM

In order to qualify themselves for the new type of citizenship made possible by the constitutional reforms, it will be necessary for Indians to reorganize the national life so as to bring it more into line with modern conditions.

They should make a careful study of the great social experiments that are being tried in various countries and introduce them wherever possible. The United States have "gone dry," and other lands are employing measures, of one kind or the other, to banish—or at any rate to regulate—drink, vice, the white-slave traffic, etc. Wholesome knowledge of sexual matters is spread broadcast by suitable literature, and confidential advice and treatment are supplied free in England. America is also setting the world a great example in getting rid of mendicancy by organizing charity. Various countries have inaugurated pensions for old persons and mothers, insurance against unemployment, sickness, and the like. Although many of these changes in their entirety may be unsuited to Indian conditions, they may yet afford suggestive guidance for wholesome and valuable changes in the country's social and economic life. India must not obstinately cling to effete practices and permit herself to lag behind.

The general outlook upon life in India, as things are now, is too gloomy to permit sound individual or social development. Far too common is the belief that life is merely a transitory stage in the passage of the soul to another world. That notion chills enthusiasm, kills joy, and promotes fatalism. The enervating climate and lack of proper nourishment react upon the nerves and accentuate the pessimistic tendency.

In some cases, the joint-family system tends to produce drones; some Indians actually take pride in the number of persons they maintain in idleness. If the person on whom the burden is placed dies, or is unable or unwilling to bear it, the dependants are left destitute, and often have to adopt mendicancy for a means of livelihood. Society should take immediate measures to put a stop to this degenerating state of affairs. Begging ought to be prohibited by law, as in Japan, and a suitable allowance made for indigent persons by the State and local authorities or civic organizations. Persons suffering from blindness, sickness, mental disease and other infirmities are better cared for in institutions specially maintained for them. In particular, institutions should be provided for defective or friendless children, facilities afforded for medical examination in schools, and, where necessary, separate hospital treatment for those little ones who require it.

While Indians feel that life is a burden, people in the West are full of hope and intensely active. They believe that the world is capable of indefinite improvement, and have faith in individual and collective effort. In India, too, with education and the new possibilities of responsible Government, the inherited pessimism of the people will gradually be dispelled by the new forces of Hope and Faith for the future.

Indians not only have a morbid outlook upon life, but are divided into rigid groups known as castes and sub-castes. Social distinctions exist in every country—distinctions based upon wealth, birth, or occupation. No country outside India has, however, a social system which cuts at the very root of human brotherhood, condemns millions of persons to perpetual degradation, makes people hyper-exclusive, magnifies religious differences, and disorganizes society.

The Indian social system has been particularly harsh upon the pariahs and so-called lower classes or "untouchables," estimated to number over 50,000,000 persons or more. As the name indicates, their very shadow is considered contaminating. They are kept in a state of abject submission and helplessness. Their education is far more neglected than that of the higher castes.

The fair Aryan hoped, by means of the caste system, to keep his stock untainted by intermixture with the dark Dravidians. The Sanskrit term for caste—*varna* (colour)—bears eloquent testimony to this origin.

Perhaps Nemesis led the Aryans in course of time to divide themselves first upon the basis of occupation, and later of birth. The desire to form separate groups for self-protection and religious worship became a potent agent in multiplying divisions.

Whatever its origin, caste enters into every detail of individual life, and everywhere plays havoc with it. Considerable time and energy is consumed in conforming to its requirements and progress above a certain standard rendered impossible.

Marriage is not permitted outside strictly prescribed limits, though during recent years more and more individuals are defying such regulations. The division into sub-castes has, indeed, proceeded so far that often it is difficult to find suitable brides. There have even been cases where men have had to wait for the birth of a daughter in a family of the prescribed caste before they could get married. Such limitations have often resulted in marriages between old men and young girls. Marriage, funeral and other ceremonies are made the occasions of extravagance, and families thereby cripple themselves and have to scrimp and scrape for years and even for life.

Boys and girls, especially among the higher castes, marry prematurely. They are physically too immature at that age to lead a married life, and they themselves and their offspring are thereby greatly handicapped in the struggle for existence.

The re-marriage of widows is regarded by high caste people as improper. Progressive persons are, however, more and more contravening conventionality in this respect.

Even though there are millions of widows, many of them of child-bearing age, and an inordinately high rate of mortality due to poor sanitary arrangements, low nourishment and famine, the population is increasing at a more rapid rate than material production.

In addition to all these marital evils

produced by the social structure peculiar to India, caste regulations interdict foreign travel. This seems strange when it is remembered that in ancient times Hindus were a great sea-faring people, trading with distant countries and even possessing colonies.

Unfortunately, many among those Indians who brave the wrath of their community and go across the "black water" (*kala pani*) are coolies who do not raise India in foreign estimation. Even many educated Indians who go abroad do not understand foreign habits, because society is so constituted that whatever changes are effected must be made stealthily. Yet, strange to say, the educated classes are copying the Western habit of drinking, and the consumption of alcoholic liquors is on the increase. With the growth of an urban population and the undermining of old beliefs, vice has shown a strong tendency to spread.

As shown by the census, literacy among women in all classes falls far below that among men. This is due to prejudices engendered by tradition, which condemns women to be economically dependent upon men, makes it impossible for them to engage in any profession other than that of a housewife, and in some parts of the country even compels them to observe strict *purdah*, and lead a secluded life.

Since the time of Raja Ram Mohan Roy, progressive Indians have sought to free society from these evils. Their efforts, however, have not fructified as they should have done; firstly, because of the appalling illiteracy prevailing in the country, especially among the women, and secondly, because Government, not being of the people, could not themselves seriously undertake social reform, and at times even felt constrained to discourage Indian reformers from doing so. Nor has the department of education sought to inculcate healthy and stimulating ideals in the rising generation. The Government has, indeed, tried to teach the people to be humble and contented with a state of subordination, with the result that India drifts as a rudderless boat on an uncharted ocean.

No extensive social reconstruction is possible unless a vigorous and systematic effort is made to banish illiteracy from the land, and the people, especially women, are given education which will broaden their outlook upon life, make them shake off lethargy, and rouse in them the ambition to better their condition.

While the right type of education will automatically do much, a special effort, a comprehensive social campaign, is indispensable for the speedy removal of the nation's handicaps.

Since caste is responsible for most of the social disorders from which India suffers, a special attempt should be made to render the system more elastic.

The caste regulations in regard to marriage, especially, need to be relaxed. While inter-racial marriages may be objected to by some persons, religion or caste should not constitute a bar to marriage. This reform would be facilitated if the central legislature would, as soon as possible, pass a law removing all civil disabilities which at present stand in the way of such unions.

While good legislation can accomplish much, the reform of society cannot be brought about by the mere passage of laws. The leaders of the various communities will not only have to carry on a vigorous propaganda against prejudicial customs, but also set worthy examples for the people to follow.

So long as enlightened men continue to marry their children prematurely, it is hopeless to expect that early marriage, as an institution, will disappear from the country. Girls should not be married earlier than sixteen, nor men before they are twenty-two years of age. Men and women in Western countries marry somewhat later still in life, but at least for the present, there should be two or three years' difference in favour of India, to allow for existing prejudices (right or wrong) and climatic conditions.

There can be no objection to the existing practice of the betrothal of girls at any age after twelve, provided that consummation of marriage is legally deferred until the age of sixteen, and provided also that the death of either party to the contract leaves the other party free to remarry.

If early marriages were stopped, there would be fewer widows in India; and the superstition which prevents the re-marriage of widows would be less keenly felt. Both common justice and prudence require that the evils of enforced widowhood and its attendant inhumanities and barbarous practices be removed.

An entirely new status should be accorded to women. The time has come when Indians must seriously consider whether the passive life, to which they condemn women with a view to preserving the so-called proprieties and decencies of life, is worth the appalling price the country is forced to pay in the shape of loss of work and intelligent effort from half the population of the country.

Indian women must be given the opportunity to acquire the highest forms of education. If they are trained to enter congenial professions, and given special facilities for obtaining profitable employment, their economic position and, with it, their status will be improved.

Similarly, the position of the "untouchables,"—i.e., persons whose very touch is deemed pollution by the caste people,—should be improved socially, educationally, and economically. Much will depend upon material prosperity, for nothing levels social position so effectively as economic success. If the lower classes are given the opportunity to amass wealth, members of higher castes will serve under them, their status will inevitably be improved and they will be able to associate in public and social functions with the upper classes.

The very idea of interfering with caste canons will doubtless be viewed with horror by every pious Hindu who has chosen to isolate himself from the rest of the world. He should, however, remember that the permanent interests of the country demand that all artificial barriers to progress should be removed.

As a matter of fact, in some respects the caste regulations are already being disregarded. Medicine, ice and aerated waters, bread and biscuits, are used without question by high-caste people who nevertheless consider that water, if touched by a low-caste person, conveys pollution. If Indians were consistent, they would consider that clean water and clean food may be accepted from any clean person's hand. If this were done, a saner social system would be built up and the business of the country would be improved.

If the country is to move forward at a rapid pace, Indians must increasingly disregard caste restrictions, break bread with one another and cultivate habits of international intercourse. Before leaving India, however, they should be taught European habits and customs. In Japan, such training is provided by Government to emigrants.

Upon their return, Indians should be freely admitted into their caste and much should be made of them, so as to learn modern ways from them and to encourage others to travel and see the world for themselves.

Unless India is willing to adopt many of the institutions, practices and habits which promote business and benefit society in other lands, she cannot hope to advance. These include regular hours of work in all business places, appreciation of the value of time, punctuality in attendance, standard habits of association, a spirit of service and co-operation, and the proprieties to be observed in conversation, in business relations, at table, and at social functions.

Standards of social functions should be prepared. As far as possible, everything that is good and noble in Indian tradition and life should be preserved, and new practices grafted upon it. The basis of behaviour should be sincerity, honesty, and utility.

Religion, the root of all social practices in India, has become a mere matter of form or ritual rather than a way of life. Indians must learn to associate high principles, character, morality and discipline as essential parts of their creed.

Small prayer books should be prepared

by every religious denomination. These should include rules governing morality and conduct, formulated with a view to inculcating a spirit of service to fellow-beings, discipline, patriotism, clean life, and clean practices, tolerance and adherence to principle.

Morality should be taught in every school from the lowest to the highest, just as ethics forms one of the principal subjects in the Japanese curriculum. The more rigid practices should, of course, be left for each individual to decide for himself or herself, but moral teachings should certainly be introduced into daily prayers.

A question of the greatest importance at the present time is on what lines social discipline shall be developed among the Indian population.

The older class of Indians complain that Western education is undermining discipline and reverence to authority. But are not such phenomena always observable in societies which are undergoing fundamental changes?

In all European countries, ever since the beginning of the modern era, precisely similar complaints have been rife.

When old systems begin to fail, when the priesthood loses its position of authority and social sanctions give way, it is inevitable that the elders and established guides should look on with apprehension lest society, without the props so long relied upon, should go to pieces and personal and domestic morality, in particular, be destroyed. Such lamentations have never been more frequent than since the close of the War.

In Western countries to-day, the central problem is to work out a system of co-operative discipline in school, college, office and factory. Some notable examples of such experiments are to be found in the schemes adopted in the Pestalozzian and Montessori schools, self-government in the higher schools, mutual aid and self-governing responsibility in the institutions for delinquent youth, and similar experiments in American prisons. Also in the joint Industrial Councils of employers and employed, the scheme of complete self-government tried in the English building trade, and the rapid spread of the national guild idea.

Unquestioning respect for authority is plainly declining in Western countries. For one thing, the bureaucratic system, grown more powerful during the War, has not increased respect for government. Employers must meet their workpeople in council. Parents must give their children reasons. Women claim equality with men and have already secured equal opportunities of entry into most professions and occupations.

What of India? Her vast population and the peculiar character of her socio-religious system, now yielding—perhaps too fast—to modern forces, are said to make her problems infinitely more difficult than those of the Western world. Her climate, too, is no doubt a disadvantage and the education given to her children affords no practical preparation for life.

The Government has been apprehensive of any co-operative efforts by the people and has actively discouraged all forms of autonomous organization or societies for mutual aid.

This has had fatal results in stifling vital interest in knowledge and work among the people, and has dangerously suppressed social emotions, which are, therefore, liable from time to time to take mischievous directions.

The Press is in chains; anti-sedition laws flourish; the young minds in college and school learn nothing of the real facts of national developments, and their thoughts dwell in a world too far from life's realities.

There is now no agency or institution with sufficient authority to utilize and develop fine Indian traditions such as the relation between teacher and pupil (*guru* and *chela*): or that wonderful conception of group loyalty which is the finer side of the caste system.

The lines on which effective organization in these and other respects can be fully developed will be discussed in a later chapter. Meanwhile, this may be said:

India must rely upon her educated young men and women to attack the great task.

Several original institutions and movements have already been initiated, such as the Anglo-Vedic College, the *Gurukula,* the Tagore school, volunteer work under Mr. Gokhale's Servants of India Society, the Calcutta volunteers, etc., although, as all these live only by sufferance, their scope is limited.

Social discipline can be easily enforced among college-educated young men, but even they will need authoritative guidance from the leading men of the country. Among the rural population, much can be done along the lines of agricultural and craft education already urged, but there is no doubt social discipline will come mainly from the development of the co-operative movement.

Among the industrial workers, it must as inevitably come through their own industrial associations.

The necessity of Indian trade unionism must be faced. The spirit of industrialism will mean the continual danger of anarchy and violence unless the employing class goes out to meet the problem frankly by peaceful methods of negotiation and conciliation. The Indian industrial workers will inevitably be organized in one of two ways: either along the aggressive lines now being pursued by the unions in Madras, or on the lines already suggested in the preceding chapter.

CHAPTER XIV

EDUCATION

When the late Prince Albert Victor, the grandson of Queen-Empress Victoria, visited the country in the 'eighties, a triumphal arch erected by the lively-witted people of the city of Poona, greeted him in these words :—

> "Tell Grandma we are a happy nation,
> But nineteen crores [1] are without education."

India to this day continues to be the land of unlettered people.

It is only necessary to compare the amount spent upon education in India with similar expenditure in other countries to understand why she lags behind progressive nations. In 1916–17, the amount spent for each 100 of the population was :—

[1] i.e., 190 million people.

Country.	Rs.
India	45
Japan	260
Great Britain	630
Canada	1,670
United States	2,700

Whereas the population attending elementary schools in India was but 2·9 per cent., it was 14·3 per cent. in Japan, and 16·5 per cent. in Great Britain. If 100 is taken as an index number for India's proportion of elementary school attendance, the following significant figures emerge :—

CHILDREN AT SCHOOL.

Country.	~~Rs.~~ %
India	100
Japan	493
Canada	548
Great Britain	568
Australia	686
United States	803

The percentage of girl pupils at school to the total female population is much smaller than these figures would indicate. Social prejudice and lack of educational facilities are responsible for keeping women's education appallingly backward. As already emphasized, India must recognize that it is impossible to make rapid progress so long as half of the population remains illiterate and inefficient.

Such primary education as is provided is of an unpractical character. The cultivator and the craftsmen view it with disfavour, as tending to estrange their boys from their surroundings and to make them dissatisfied with their hereditary calling without necessarily fitting them for anything better.

Secondary and university education, though producing many able recruits for subordinate positions in the Civil Service, does not provide the men needed to carry on the work of agriculture, engineering, commerce and technology. The provision for training in economics and history is inadequate, and the study of those subjects is even discouraged. An attempt is actually made to teach economics in such a way as to render India's emergence from a state of dependency difficult.

The fees charged for education in the

higher branches are exorbitant, and the scholarships are too few. In consequence, a mass of talent in humble circumstances is left undeveloped and even unsuspected. The policy of increasing fees in order to meet increasing expenditure will defeat its own ends.

Britain herself has had to pay a heavy price for her hand-to-mouth policy in regard to education. The educational chaos still existing there compares unfavourably with the great yet orderly progress made by Germany and Japan, both of which countries, after weighing and testing the educational systems of the world, absorbed the best of all.

Now that a beginning is about to be made in responsible government in India, it is necessary that the standard of education should be such as to fit the people to exercise the powers and responsibilities of citizenship, and to take full advantage of the social and economic opportunities which are opening before them.

India may advantageously follow in respect of education the example set by Japan. That country, though not so very long ago as backward as India is to-day, has so raised her standard of education as to ensure a steady growth of progress and prosperity.

Another lesson in this respect has been provided by the enterprise shown by the Americans in educating the Filipinos, who in twenty years have advanced far ahead of Indians in percentage of literacy. The system of education introduced into the Philippines, moreover, lays great stress upon vocational teaching, and therefore conduces to rapid economic development.

Within the next ten years, India's education budget should approximate £25,000,000, allocated as follows :—

Branch of Education.	Scholars.	Proportion per 1,000 of the total population of B. India (260,000,000)	Cost in million £.
Elementary Schools	36,400,000	140	18
Secondary Schools .	3,640,000	14	3·5
Universities . . .	390,000	1·5	3·0
Special Education .	130,000	·5	·5
	40,560,000	156	25

Deducting the present total expenditure of £7,500,000, and assuming that another £7,500,000 will be met by local governing bodies, there will remain a deficiency of £10,000,000, which will have to be met partly by increased taxation and partly by means of a loan. The unproductive debt of India is very small. Government should not hesitate to add to it such a profitable investment as an education loan.

Expenditure on education, like labour expended upon tilling and fertilizing the soil, will repay itself many fold. Since the nation will reap the first-fruits of this harvest, the increasing outlay upon education should, in the main, be a national charge. The fees should be merely nominal, and the scholarships sufficient in number really to encourage talent and endeavour.

Every provincial Government should develop its educational department and appoint a Minister of Education. That department should be in close touch with every city, town, and even village, which should also have education councils or committees to carry on local work, and to become centres of thought and enlightenment in every branch of education and self-improvement, whether for young people or adults. Such committees should maintain some sort of institute, with a reading-room, lecture-room, and at least the nucleus of a reference library.

The education council of the city or town should be a very important body with far-reaching influences. It might consist of representatives of the provincial Government, the local authority, the nearest university, and any education or recreative associations, and should include professors, teachers and wage-earners, while some members might be co-opted from among distinguished men and women.

The educational institute, in addition to library, reading-rooms and lecture-hall, might include a museum, concert-hall and possibly even a theatre. Professors and teachers should be given the opportunity to visit other districts and provinces, and conferences should be held from time to time for the exchange of views.

Each large village should have at least one primary school. Smaller villages might be grouped for this purpose, after the fashion of the combinations of rural school-districts in some parts of the United States.

It is necessary to formulate a programme of national education along broad, well-conceived lines, and with something like deliberate choice of the means best adapted to the desired end.

Commencing with education broad-based on the nation's childhood, no doubt something like 90 per cent. of the school population would attend the primary schools. In that case, instead of the present elementary school attendance of 6,000,000, India should have 35,000,000 boys and girls attending primary schools, later to emerge with at least sufficient mental equipment to give them alertness, self-confidence, and eagerness to improve and progress.

The school-life should extend from five or six to twelve years of age. The elementary course should comprise the "three R's" and, in addition, such subjects as drawing, nature-study and the elements of business morals, especially the necessity of discipline in all realms of life, the value of time, and behaviour towards elders.

Linked with the elementary school system, there should be "vocational" schools, to provide training in the elements of agriculture, commerce, handicrafts, carpentry, engineering, woodwork, smithing, and other trades for the boys, and cookery, dressmaking, nursing and housewifery for girls. Probably 60 per cent. of the boys in rural areas would require agricultural training. Where a vocational school is not possible, arrangements might be made for the requisite subjects to be taught in continuation classes on special week-days or, perhaps, in the evenings.

Pupils going direct from elementary to secondary schools need not take the primary vocational or continuation course. Since probably not more than 10 per cent. of the children would pass to the secondary schools, the vocational course would follow in most cases, continuing for perhaps two to four years according to the subjects and the pupil's intelligence.

Most cities and towns should be secondary school centres, admission to the secondary school being secured either by means of a scholarship, or by payment of a reasonable fee.

Four to six years in the secondary school should arouse in the student an intelligent interest in the affairs of everyday life, and, in a measure at least, make him clean thinking and clean living, cultivate his powers of observation and generalization, develop in him such elementary virtues as industry, thrift and voluntary co-operation with his fellows, awaken his innate sense of citizenship and public spirit, and give him a good general grounding for his future career. The practical subjects taught should include civil and mechanical engineering, technology, agriculture, commercial methods, medicine, cabinet-making, pottery, handloom-weaving, dressmaking, metal work, leather work and other handicrafts and practical workshop trades, especially those connected with house-building.

These practical courses should not in any way interfere with the liberal education. Both should go hand in hand, or a general education might be followed by a special vocational course, in which theory and practice would be developed concurrently.

In many cases a student well qualified to proceed from the secondary school to the university, but unable to take advantage of a full university course, may yet be able to devote a certain amount of time to higher studies. To meet such cases, the universities should assist the local education authorities to provide training in the more immediate and practical phases of "higher" education. Voluntary agencies would undoubtedly be found willing to assist in affording such opportunities, as is the case in Japan and other countries.

In addition to the usual professional and commercial subjects, such university extension courses might include languages, finance, natural science, music, painting, etc. The object of such classes should be to enable students to qualify themselves to take a leading part in a specific trade, art, or profession.

The disadvantages of a purely literary education are so apparent that many great rulers have caused their sons and daughters to be trained in practical trades and handicrafts. This is always done in the case of the children of the British Royal Family. Cities in the United States and Canada show much enterprise in providing commercial and technical education. It behoves Indian cities to do likewise.

The university should, of course, aim particularly at developing leaders, governors, thinkers, administrators and directors for every branch of political, social, commercial and industrial activities. Among the subjects taught should be medicine, architecture, civil, mechanical and electrical engineering, chemistry, mining and metallurgy, scientific agriculture, forestry, ship-building, economics, finance and statistics. The subjects which will give the best results for the country at present are commerce and mechanical engineering and technology.

Within the next five years, the number of universities should be raised from the seven now in existence to about twenty. Official control should be entirely withdrawn, and, as in Canada, each university made a self-governing institution with provincial support.

Every province should also provide for the maintenance in progressive countries of bands of students, who should pursue advanced studies in some particular branch of industry or carry on research work. These students should be selected from those who had acquitted themselves well in commercial and industrial subjects, chemistry, economics, civics, sociology and other courses. In addition to special training for research work, it should be necessary for them to have mastered a foreign language such as French, German, or Japanese. The provincial Governments should at first find one-half of the money required for this foreign travel and study.

But for the work done by the Japanese trained abroad, dyeing, tanning, oils and fats, paper-making, machinery, glass, porcelain and pottery, and other industries would not have made the phenomenal progress which has been achieved. If India is to go forward, she must follow the Japanese example in these respects.

Schools for the blind, the deaf and dumb, and other defectives, will no doubt be established as adjuncts to general education, as soon as the new educational machinery is set in motion.

The development of ordinary and special education in India depends largely upon the effort put into the work of training teachers. The facilities for this purpose at present existing are utterly inadequate, while the character of normal instruction leaves much to be desired. The salaries paid to teachers are much too low to attract the right type of men and women to the profession.

Both the Government and the people must recognize that only by pursuing a liberal educational policy, and making generous financial provision for schools and colleges can they lift India out of her present low condition and ensure rapid progress.

Shaping the Future

CHAPTER XV

NATION-BUILDING

Do the people of India propose to profit by the lessons which world experience has to teach them, or will they be content to allow matters to drift and themselves grow weaker and poorer year by year ?

This is the problem of the hour. They have to choose whether they will be educated or remain ignorant ; whether they will come into closer touch with the outer world and become responsive to its influences, or remain secluded and indifferent ; whether they will be organized or disunited, bold or timid, enterprising or passive ; an industrial or an agricultural nation ; rich or poor ; strong and respected, or weak and dominated by forward nations. The future is in their own hands. Action, not sentiment, will be the determining factor.

Nations are made by their own efforts. No nation can shape the life of another. It has been said that the politician, the sociologist and the educator should put their heads together and determine the kind of world they wish to create, and then order the processes accordingly. It should be easy for India, if she made the effort on an adequate scale along lines suggested by world-experience, to will the character of her future, and so to shape that future that, like Canada and Australia, she will soon become a self-governing unit within the British Empire.

The United Kingdom, for instance, as was recently stated by Mr. Lloyd George, is more than four-fifths industrial and commercial and one-fifth agricultural. The country does not grow its own food, but concentrates its attention upon industry, commerce, ship-building and ocean freight, economic exploitation, and ruling the weaker and backward races. It finds this form of activity to be more remunerative, and provides an incomparably higher standard of comfort for the nation than if the manhood of the country remained at home and grew crops. There are risks, of course, in following such a national policy. Political hostilities may be roused, food supply may run short, and emergencies of one sort or another may arise: but the country faces the risks with courage and determination, because of the great advantages and high standard of living assured by its present policy.

Japan is closely following the example of the United Kingdom. Already her production from industry is double that from agriculture, and her commerce is growing rapidly.

The United States of America and Canada, on the other hand, are so vast in area and so replete with resources and opportunities, that they have no incentive to acquire more land for the sake of providing lucrative employment for their people. On the contrary, they are inviting immigrants to settle there with a view to increasing production and profits. They have developed agriculture and industry to a high level of efficiency, and as they want markets for the products of both, they are now, particularly since the close of the War, extending their shipping industry and foreign trade.

While the rest of the world has been forging forward, India has been standing still. Her resources in materials have remained undeveloped. Her administration, industry and trade have been so organized that they have given but scant opportunities for the employment and development of the talent and energy of the people of the soil.

Experience shows that a nation is the most effective unit of combination for securing to the people composing it the maximum benefit from their aggregate activities and efforts. Scattered communities cannot benefit themselves or their country. In order to develop the political and economic strength possessed by the Dominions, India must in future cherish and develop a spirit of nationhood. Ex-President Taft, of the United States of America, has said :—

"I believe in nationality and patriotism, as distinguished from universal brotherhood, as firmly as any one. I believe that a nation spirit and patriotic love of country are as essential in the progress o the world as the family and the love of family are essential in domestic communities."

Addressing the International Congress of Philosophy at Oxford so recently as September 27th last, Mr. A. J. Balfour claimed that nationality lent itself more than any other system to modern development, and to all the complex interests of a very highly complex modern community. He thought that among all forms of producing human co-operation, the best way of getting a full democratic constitution was through the principle, as far as they could develop it, of nationality.

India must develop the idea of nationality; and endeavour to organize and work out her national destiny along broad lines. Love of country should be encouraged, for India as a whole as well as for the provinces, the city, town, or village of residence. By means of suitable propaganda, pride should be cultivated in all good and great things inherited from the past, and enthusiasm to raise the country from good to better as years go by. Love of fellow-men and pride in national leaders, both past and present, should be inculcated. The individual citizen must be made to understand that in helping his fellow-men he is doing good to himself, the country as a whole, and to succeeding generations of his countrymen. By organization and united effort every individual and the nation collectively will gain. The lesson for India from world experience in this respect is that she can promote her interests only by working after the example of the Dominions as a united nation.

A nation that goes counter to world-experience and world-standards is bound to bring about its own ruin. This is what is happening in India. Sound economic laws are being transgressed, and the experience of foreign countries is being ignored. The lines on which the country should advance in future are quite clear. If Indians do what ten other nations have done successfully, they cannot possibly go wrong. Where the Government helps them in their objects and plans, the public should render whole-hearted co-operation. Where the Government fails to act, the people should have an independent policy and organizations of their own to accomplish their object by their own effort, making the most of the opportunities open to them.

A nation is a super-combination of organizations consisting of the leading men of the country and large sections of the population engaged in various occupations, held together by mutual interest and the authority and influence of Government.

The Government and the people usually supplement each other's efforts in policy, organization and production; and the object of establishing national organizations with the Government at the apex of the system, is to increase political power, national industry and social betterment. As the aims of the leaders of the people and of Government are not identical in India, there are at present no organizations common to both for promoting the general welfare. If the country had a definite scheme of national life, and definite national programmes which commanded the confidence of the majority of the people, individuals and associations would be able to shape their own activities in accordance therewith. As it is, the absence of common ideals has led in local areas to inaction and stagnation and much misdirected and unproductive effort.

To avoid this waste in future, a definite move should be made towards building up an Indian nation by outlining national plans and programmes in the political, economic and social spheres. An attempt has been made in previous pages to indicate the character of the national plans necessary to deal with India's reconstruction problems.

If the Government helps in the work of nation-building, the British nation will rise in the estimation of Indians, and will win their deepest gratitude. It is, however, too much to hope that the Government, as at present constituted, will do much in this direction. This being so, the people must prepare for themselves a programme of reconstruction that will advance their own national interests.

The speediest way for Indians to win complete responsible Government is to deserve it and work for it. If they expect to receive it as a gift from the British Government, it will be very slow in coming.

Canada experienced the same difficulties. The British officials there considered themselves the custodians of Imperial responsibilities and at first opposed the growth of the nationalist sentiment. What followed may be stated in the words of Sir Robert Borden, the late Premier of that Dominion :—

" Step by step the Colonies have advanced towards the position of virtual independence as far as their internal affairs are concerned, and in all the important instances the claim that has been made by Canada has been resisted at first by the Imperial statesmen and finally conceded, proving an advantage both to the Mother Country and the Colonists."

Writing in *The New Era in Canada*, Mr. John W. Dafoe, a well-known journalist, observes :—

" Influences radiating from London have sought from time to time to check or discourage the march forward of Canadian nationalism in the supposed interests of the Empire, and these have never lacked the zealous co-operation of strong Canadian groups in Canada. Experience has shown, however, that, despite the strength of the ultra-British group, the programme of national Canadianism goes forward, and a position once occupied is never lost."

The best method of national activity should be selected. This will be possible only if delegations of Indian statesmen, students and business men are sent abroad to study up-to-date foreign systems, theories and practices.

Such a plan has been followed by Japan ever since she set her feet upon the path of modernization. Men and women students were sent by the Government to every country in the world to study foreign institutions, educational methods, jurisprudence and social relations. The information they carried back with them was pooled, and from it were selected the methods which, it was felt, were best suited to Japanese requirements. These were made the bases of national policies. As Professor W. A. Osborne said in a speech recently delivered in Ottawa, referring to the presence of Japanese students in Canada :—

"They (the Japanese students) were not there (in Canada) in a purely personal capacity . . . they were there as part of a great body of the chosen youth of Japan who had been sent out from that country to rifle the intellectual resources of the countries to which they were accredited or sent in the interests of their own nation. That is to say, their Government practically hand-picked those men and sent them out to study. . . . That was a great national scheme, and I have not the slightest doubt that it was the eclectic educational methods that Japan adopted thirty or forty years ago . . . that enabled Japan to pass so quickly from the rank of a hermit feudal state into the rank of a first-class power, with which even Great Britain was proud to make an alliance."

India must develop a type of national life suited to her circumstances and aspirations. She desires to be a self-governing Dominion like Canada—to possess autonomy within her own borders, and to be allowed to co-operate for defence and development with Great Britain and other self-governing units within the British Empire. Such a type of national life will be impossible unless the people are taught to unite, and to fraternize for the promotion of essential objects of interest common to large areas of the country and to India as a whole. The discordant elements among the population must be gradually harmonized. They should learn to acquire the spirit of unselfish service and of responsibility for the public good.

The process of unifying the tastes and mentality of a population differing in race, religion and language, by means of education and training, is at present going on in the United States of America, where the heterogeneous immigrants who have gone there from all parts of Europe are being "Americanized." Acting on the same principle, India must recognize that certain standards of taste, thought and sentiment are necessary to union, and should devise and carry out a comprehensive scheme of "Indianization," with a view to creating a new type of Indian citizenship and building up an efficient unified Indian nation.

The principal characteristics to be developed in the life and habits of the people under an "Indianization" programme should, in essential, be as follows :—

(1) Love and pride of country (nation, province, city, town, or village); a high sense of self-respect and

personal honour, and a spirit of service, combined with loyalty to the Sovereign and to the British connection.

(2) Use of a common language in every province, and of English as the *lingua franca.*

(3) A minimum of six years' compulsory general education, and a further two to four years' vocational course for every boy and girl, due attention being paid to games and sports and physical development, and to moral discipline.

(4) Training in civics and thrift in schools, and, for adults, in special institutions, or by lectures and cinemas.

(5) Organized effort to eradicate unhealthy ideals and practices known to handicap the Indian and to standardize existing good traits, practices and traditions in the country, and protect them from disuse or decay.

(6) Cultivation of a spirit of initiative and

habits of closer association; uniformity of dress, as far as possible; acquisition of business discipline and the usages of civilization; travel among all classes of people, including the establishment of hotels and better railway facilities for the middle and poorer classes.

(7) Equipping all classes of the people with correct ideals and objectives to work for, so that individual and local effort may be in consonance with national objects and aspirations.

(8) Training all leading men and women to take part in international life and intercourse.

In order that individual and collective citizenship may be developed, the Indian people must be equipped with a general knowledge of the conditions of success, with skill in some profession or trade to enable them to earn a living, and with sufficient character and discipline to harmonize human relations and promote co-operative effort.

The manner and rate of national development will depend upon the opportunities for training enjoyed by the people, and the extent to which they avail themselves of such facilities and submit to discipline.

Most well-informed persons will agree that a stimulus is necessary if new habits and practices are to be introduced into the country. Some of the suggestions made in this book will be distasteful to a section of the public on account of the exertion and discipline they will demand. Others will object to them because they run counter to their cherished traditions and prejudices. To others, again, some of the changes, such as common dining, suggested for the great majority of the population, may seem revolutionary. It must be remembered, however, that the interests at stake are very great, that world ideals are shifting very fast, and that responsible government demands a new type of citizenship.

The characteristics to be developed in the Indian population should form a subject of earnest study by all politicians, business men, sociologists and educationists interested in Indian progress. A committee or board of leading men should be appointed in each province to study this important question, and to recommend, within a period of one year, definite standards and methods for the guidance of the people. This committee should refer the subjects and correlated questions to persons qualified to give advice both within and without the province, and representative Indians residing outside India. A symposium of the opinions elicited may be collected and published along with the committee's own recommendations. The "Indianization" proposals should be printed in English and in the vernacular of each province, and should be brief and have literary finish, so that they may be attractive and readily referred to. Each province may have its own "Indianization" scheme, but the recommendations of one province, although intended for practice in that particular province, should be available for study and comparison in all the other provinces.

The tentative "Indianization" programme approved by the committee may be recommended for adoption and practice from the date of issue. It may be revised once every year for the first three years, and after that period once every three years. A revision at intervals will be necessary to adapt it to the changing conditions of the outer world; but after two or three revisions, it may be assumed that the standard will change but slightly, only yielding to acknowledged world changes.

The people should be persuaded, by means of effective organization and otherwise, to practise the standards prescribed by the leaders. An essential characteristic of every such organization should be its healthy spirit of self-improvement and self-development.

CHAPTER XVI

ORGANIZATION

India is very weak in organization. In small matters connected with religion, caste, social practices, etc., the people have preserved some remnants of their old organization; but in other directions, particularly in the control of economic matters affecting the material well-being of the people, such as industry, trade, transportation, banking, etc., it has been seen that whatever organization exists is British. Independent indigenous organizations of any magnitude have had no chance.

Regarding the need of organization in India, a well-known Bombay journal, the *Indian Social Reformer*, observed in 1912 :—

"There is nothing in which we in this country need to be instructed so much as in organization, whether of industry, education, or charity, or even political activity. Organization is, broadly speaking, such a disposition of the energies and resources of the community as to enable them to be rapidly mobilized and concentrated on the points where they are most wanted or can be most useful. There is plenty of almost everything in this country, but one great defect is that nothing is where it should be, and everything is so dispersed that it is almost impossible to bring it when and where it is wanted. Thus in the midst of plenty we have often to starve."

Nothing really large, however, is ever done without organization, and the strength of organization in any particular country depends upon its political condition. In democratic countries like England or America, most organizations owe their origin to popular initiative. Government is always anxious to render help to public organizations and earn their good opinion, because the personnel of the Government owe their position to the support of the people. In India, where the people's support counts for nothing, the work of organization for any public purpose beyond a certain stage is difficult and oftentimes impossible. In countries like Japan, which have their own national Government, the initiative in this respect chiefly comes from

Government, which is composed of a few far-sighted statesmen chosen from the people. On account of the paternal character of the administration, the public in that country have willingly surrendered their interests into the hands of an oligarchy.

Organization for a country like India is the process of arranging or combining the constituent parts into a co-ordinated whole, and of utilizing the working forces of the country to produce the most desired composite effect. This is true also of local organizations. As was observed in a paper recently issued by the Washington State Board of Commerce:—

> "Community organizations have already been recognized as a necessity to any community which expects to grow to any great degree, but with the changing conditions in this country brought about by its rapid development on the one hand and the great changes due to the recent War on the other, community organizations are now recognized as an essential part of every town and city. Such an organization provides a medium through which the citizens of a community may pool their best efforts and ideas for the welfare of the community, for its expansion as a trading or industrial centre, and particularly to bring into the community life those things which will promote true . . . citizenship."

Every organization or association, according to the latest practice, must have working members and supporters, an adequate income, a competent secretary and working staff, a good office system, a definite programme of work, specific rules for committee formation and control, an agency for publicity and propaganda and intelligent local service.

When an association or society is organized for a public purpose, the executive and the members proceed to collect the necessary information and data, and study and discuss among themselves the subject or subjects connected with their purpose. The study and discussions lead to a common understanding on many points and to the clarification of issues on doubtful ones. The doubtful points are then discussed and decisions and conclusions formed by a majority, large or small. The next step commonly taken is to act on the decisions. The three stages of the work of an organization therefore are: (1) study; (2) decision; and (3) action. Where an organization is effective, all three stages are covered very quickly.

Unanimous decisions are reached only in matters which are obvious to everybody. Decisions are usually taken according to the opinion of the majority and these are, or have to be, acquiesced in by the whole body, to enable the organization to proceed to the next stage in the case.

The number of subjects which crowd upon the attention of any particular organization being usually very large, the selection of subjects for treatment from the large mass of problems and indefinite alternatives which distract attention is a difficult matter. Skill and forethought are necessary to concentrate attention upon the essential and the attainable.

In this work of selection, the people would be wise to be guided not only by British examples, but by the varied experiences of all the progressive countries of the world. For many local problems in India, ready-made solutions will be available in countries like Canada and Japan. It is not wise to attempt to create a new world for ourselves by shutting our eyes to the experience already accumulated by the mistakes and patient labour of the people of other lands.

In connection with every organization, continuity of purpose and policy should be held in view. A clear record must be kept of the decisions and schemes determined upon in every branch of the country's activity. From month to month and year to year, new decisions will be taken and new practices introduced and new codes of decisions built up and many of them translated into action. The accumulation of practical results in this way, of work done, decisions accepted, rules and practices codified, will constitute an asset indicative of the true development and progress of the country.

Propaganda is the means resorted to by individuals and public bodies for popularizing national ideals and programmes; spreading useful information; promoting organization and co-operation for general or specific objects; bringing to notice defects and wants and inviting opinions and action thereon; rousing enthusiasm for any public reform or scheme, and promoting any object of public interest whatever, temporary or permanent. Propaganda will be necessary to educate the public or to secure popular support for, or stimulate dynamic effort in, any public cause.

It takes the form of a campaign or drive, when it is undertaken in an emergency to accomplish a specific object or purpose within a given time.

Propaganda was resorted to for correcting wrong impressions and spreading reliable information during the late War. It might be most beneficially utilized in India in the coming years for popularizing national plans and programmes and training the people for full responsible government.

Among the principal propaganda agencies are public meetings and periodical gatherings. An agency even more important is the Press. Newspapers have a three-fold object—supplying news, publishing advertisements and instructing the public with opinions and comments on current questions. Where they are not worked in a purely commercial spirit or in the interests of a class, they do much good by ventilating public grievances, by rousing public opinion and stimulating activity on the part of both public associations and the Government.

Propaganda is carried on by magazines, booklets, pamphlets, leaflets, folders, etc., and also by public notices, placards and posters, often exhibited on street walls, in tramcars and railway carriages.

In future every public election, whether for Imperial, provincial or local councils, should be taken advantage of for purposes of propaganda.

Cinemas might be used for spreading sound ideas on such subjects as civic life, housing, sanitation, industries, etc. Indigenous professional reciters and musicians, whose normal vocation is to recite stories from ancient epics, may be most effectively employed on propagandist work. As is done in other parts of the world, the professors of Indian universities and colleges should be free to instruct the public. Short treatises like the *Oxford Tracts* will be serviceable if written by university professors whose view of current problems will be disinterested and whose motives, therefore, will be above suspicion.

The extent to which propaganda is resorted to in this way in any public cause, and the persistence with which the work is continued, will be an indication of the earnestness of the people concerned, and of their capacity to build up unity of thought and action in the country.

Public associations in India might adopt the business methods of the West more scrupulously and carry on propaganda in a more active spirit than is done at present. Some of the existing associations in the country are badly managed through inattention to discipline and the omission to collect funds to maintain a good secretary and effective staff. Meetings are irregular, subscriptions are in arrears, one or a few persons monopolize the whole responsibility, and reports and accounts are not rendered punctually.

Associations get into a rut and growth is prevented where the whole responsibility is monopolized by one or two persons. The originators of associations should ever be seeking for others upon whom they can throw work and responsibility, thus at the same time broadening their own mental outlook and the sphere of influence of the association. Constant touch should be kept with the rank and file of the members through widespread local committees, each with its own officers. Every member should be made to feel that he is a valued unit of the association and given some office or responsibility directly he reveals any special capacity.

As public opinion will receive recognition and consideration from Government in future, popular associations will vastly increase their influence. They will begin to feel what a useful part they can play in public affairs and realize their responsibility for efficient operation.

In the immediate future the aim of the Indian leaders should be to keep the people thinking and working; to rouse in them a spirit of development and progress;

increase their scale of combination and organization; and until complete responsible government is conceded, to maintain a separate unifying agency or agencies independent of Government in order to secure continuity of purpose and policy, and unity of direction in regard to all affairs and activities of a national character.

For securing unity of direction, it will be found an advantage to hold a few reliable men responsible for a fixed term at a time for the production of results and to change the men at regular intervals so as to avoid the common faults of Indian organizations, viz., slackness of effort or autocracy.

For the purpose of organization, the whole country may be marked out into seven spheres or regions, thus: (1) All India, (2) province, (3) city, (4) town, (5) village, (6) district, (7) sub-district (*taluk*).

For the sake of uniformity, the entire activities of the country may be divided into three classes, as has been done in this book: viz. (1) political and administrative, (2) economic, and (3) social. The proposals under the "Indianization" scheme will come under the third head, "Social."

In any area coming under any one of these seven spheres or regions, the leading inhabitants interested may come together and start a central organizing agency to be known as the "Development Committee."

This committee should be non-political and non-partisan, and its chief business should be to bring into existence all the public associations and agencies needed in the locality according to the example of advanced countries, and to help to keep these agencies alert and active and absorbed in investigating public questions and supplying the deficiencies and wants of the region or area concerned. The development committee in any region or area will be started in the first instance by persons who desire to promote the interests of the locality, but when the region or area is equipped with all the usual organizations, the committee itself may be grouped with, and merged in, the economic organizations of the area and derive its funds and support from them. At a later stage uniform regulations may be introduced so that the development committees, wherever they may be, may all work on a common plan of organization and so eventually form a national development league: but it is not desirable to aim at such uniformity at the very start.

The reason why the development committee should be classed with economic organizations is that it has to be operated on national lines without party bias. Association with either political or social reform organizations is undesirable, since these latter deal with subjects of a controversial character and are apt to divide instead of uniting the population.

Among the essential duties of organizations in each of the seven spheres or areas may be enumerated: the preparation of succinct statements of national plans and programmes to enable the public to visualize the future; preparation and maintenance of lists of urgent and important problems; formation of study circles for investigating and elucidating the problems; frequent publication of the opinions of study circles and of symposia of views of leading men on current topics; issue of standard circulars (by recognized leading central organizations for the guidance of the public); and bringing into existence institutions and agencies needed both for thought and action in the area, one by one, according to civilized standards.

In general terms, the organizations in each sphere or area should provide for (1) the work of initiative in order to bring into existence the activities, institutions and agencies needed in the area and (2) the work of leadership to co-ordinate all the activities and ensure central control and action.

The organizations needed for (1) all India and (2) each province will be similar in character. For all India, there may be created a central council consisting of seven members and 200 associates for developing and unifying the political work of the country. This council would work in close association with the existing all-

India political organizations. The central council should prepare and maintain lists of current political and administrative questions and large problems requiring continuous attention, and it should distribute these problems among study circles formed from the 200 associates and other co-opted workers, drawn from public men, statisticians, business men, university professors, etc., throughout the country.

The central council and associated organizations and study circles will keep under study Imperial, national and international problems, and will from time to time publish the results of their study and recommendations for the information and guidance of the public. Such recommendations will be discussed at the annual sessions of political federations like the National Congress and Moslem League, and definite lines of action settled upon.

For the economic work of the whole country, a central national council of seven persons and 200 associates may be formed on similar lines. The council will work in association with the industrial conference and other economic associations in the country on the same lines.

If sufficient interest is evinced in social matters, a similar central council of seven leaders and 200 associates may be constituted also for the social work of all India on lines very similar to political and economic councils. This council will work in co-operation with the all-India social conference or congress.

For the present, at all events, it is not desirable that the same leaders should be represented on any of these three central councils for more than one year at a time, save in the case of persons who evince exceptional zeal, energy and ability and who are willing to devote most of their time to the work of the council.

In the same way every province will require three classes of central councils with 200 associates each. These provincial councils will be responsible for the work of the province for a year at a time, and will carry on their duties in consultation with the corresponding conferences and other existing provincial organizations.

For each of the remaining five spheres or areas there may be one or more associations, societies, clubs, etc., under any or all the three heads, political, economic and social. The organizations and their activities will differ in quality and scale according to local circumstances. In a city, for instance, there may be a political association, a ratepayers' association, a foreign travel association and so on. For economic work there may be a Chamber of Commerce, an economic conference, a manufacturers' association, an agricultural association, etc. For social work there may be associations for social reform, civic survey, town-planning, child welfare, education, physical culture, etc. Many of the organizations required in each area have already been mentioned in different parts of this book and need not be repeated here. It is sufficient if a correct impression is here conveyed how such associations and agencies fit in with a comprehensive organization for the whole country.

Enough has been said to enable the residents of any given sphere or area, whether it be a province or a city, town or village, or a district or sub-district, to prepare a working organization and programmes on the basis explained.

The public bodies and associations which may thus be brought into existence may be independent at first. Any city, town or village may start any association or society for which there is use in the locality and there are the men to run it. No city, town or village need wait for another to make a beginning. In due course some form of co-operation will come to be established between the various associations engaged in like activities through the provincial and central agencies. Such co-operation may be kept in view, but need not be attempted from the very start.

Some spheres or areas will require all three classes of organizations; others one or a few only; in others again, existing organizations will need supplementing. Many towns and villages, through lack of men of ability or other resources, will be unable to maintain all the organizations needed.

In each sphere there may be several organizations, sometimes rival associations, working for the same or similar objects. In such cases it is the duty of all these to come together and appoint, for short intervals at a time, a central unifying agency to work upon objects common to all of them. In a number of organizations of the same class, one of the senior organizations may be entrusted with this work, say, for a year at a time. The latter will prepare statements of wants to be provided and defects to be remedied and questions to be solved and will constitute study groups, and in some cases committees or sub-committees, in order to investigate problems that are of common interest and suggest solutions.

As public men doing honorary duties will not be able to work with the same earnestness and energy or to give the amount of time necessary for long intervals, it is enough for the present to select national and provincial central councils for one year at a time. The leaders should be selected with scrupulous care so that the public of all denominations may confide in their judgment and accept advice and recommendations coming from them. No public man, however influential, should be on the council of seven members unless he is prepared to devote a considerable portion of his time to its work during its life of twelve months. When he is replaced, he will, in the ordinary course, be brought on the list of associates and will continue to render service on the study circles and otherwise.

Under this arrangement, large numbers of persons will be engaged in the study of current problems and in keeping themselves in touch with what is happening in progressive countries. All matters of public interest will be watched and studied. The services of men of worth and ability will be utilized on the study groups, the activities needed for progress will be maintained and mass consciousness developed. All the material and spiritual powers in each area will be mobilized and energetic action throughout the whole country stimulated and sustained.

CHAPTER XVII

THE IMMEDIATE TASK

India's fundamental problem consists in relieving the soil of over-pressure of population by the development of industry, and thereby attacking at its foundation the appalling poverty which is crushing her people. Such advance is possible only if illiteracy is banished from the country and education of a practical character liberally provided, and if the social evils which obstruct progress are systematically removed.

An honest endeavour has been made in this book to state the causes which are responsible for keeping India in such a low educational, economic and social condition, and to outline the measures of reconstruction immediately needed. These may, in conclusion, be briefly summarized.

As regards education, the requisite number of primary schools should be started and compulsory attendance of all children of school age, both boys and girls, should be enforced by law. When the new education programme is in full operation, the attendance at schools in towns and villages should be not less than fifteen per cent. of the population. In cities it should be more. Persons under eighteen years of age who have to earn a living and are employed, should be required to attend continuation schools for at least six hours every week to learn some profession or occupation.

Elementary practical science as applied to agriculture and industry, elementary book-keeping and rudiments of information concerning the economic structure of the world and of India in particular, as well as instruction in the duties of citizenship, should form part of the primary school curriculum. The initial outlay on buildings and equipment and the training of teachers will be very considerable; but it is an obligation that must be met, even if money be borrowed to supplement the funds available from current revenues.

Every province should have its own university, and at least one good technical and one commercial college for every 15,000,000 population, giving the highest education in their respective subjects. Some twenty universities should be brought into existence during the next five years. Civics and economics should form obligatory subjects of study for seventy-five per cent. of the students attending the universities. Thus it will be possible to train the organizers, statesmen and leaders so badly needed at present, and for whose services, if all goes well, there will be an ever-increasing demand in future.

Each province should depute, for training in foreign countries, fifty or more students at a time—the exact number depending upon the population. Nearly half of these students should be maintained by the provincial Government. In addition, the provincial Governments should dispatch, at regular intervals, deputations of prominent Indians to Canada, Australia and Japan, and maintain agencies in those countries to supply information and answer communications from the people of the province.

A study of the political and economic framework and machinery of other countries will be of the highest value in devising schemes for building India's national life, and will save the country from many blunders; for, when ready-made models are available, it is not the part of wisdom to shut the eyes to them and resort to the costly alternative of making new experiments.

India must depend chiefly upon the development of large factory industries for creating wealth. They will also give a lead to medium-scale and minor industries. A dozen large industries, including railway supplies, machinery, motor-cars, paper, oil, porcelain, glass, leather and other articles should be started. Iron and textile manufactures should be greatly extended, and shipbuilding given special prominence.

A Board of Industries composed of Indian members and aided by British, foreign and Indian experts, should be given a free hand to direct industrial enterprises in every province, under the control of the Minister of Industries. Funds to the extent of Rs. 10,000,000 to Rs. 30,000,000 per annum should be at the disposal of each provincial Government within the next ten years for financing industries. The accounts for this expenditure may be subject to the strictest audit, but the Board, consisting of men enjoying the confidence of the provincial Legislative Council, should be free to grant all reasonable concessions to *bona fide* local business men. A research institute, experimental stations and other agencies, institutions and laboratories required, should be provided for making experiments and training organizers, works managers and the labour force of the province. Local organizers with directing ability should be sought out and given financial and other facilities and encouraged to start large concerns with the aid of experts. A reasonable measure of protection should be afforded by levying import duties to safeguard the interests of infant industries.

Five to ten years of such sympathetic and systematic encouragement would make phenomenal progress possible.

Further increase of production from agriculture will be possible if resort is had to intensive cultivation and the use of scientific methods of tillage, better farm and chemical manures and labour-saving tools and machinery. Irrigation, if extended, will prove a great source of wealth. Approved agricultural methods should be taught in experimental stations and in schools as well as by propaganda. India's salvation in this respect lies in introducing new ideas—in gradually training the farmer to develop himself from a labourer into an intelligent and self-reliant worker.

Agricultural associations, co-operative societies and banks will be needed for every town and village group. At the commencement, a deputation of half a dozen leading farmers, accompanied by one or two graduates in agriculture, should be sent every six months from each province to Europe, America and Japan.

Government agencies to protect Indian traders, and Indian banks to finance their trade, should be provided in England and in selected foreign countries. Foreign language schools should be established in the principal cities, and Indian-owned shipping encouraged to facilitate foreign intercourse.

A review of the position of Indians in foreign countries, accompanied by reliable statistics, should be prepared and published as a necessary preliminary to the development of this phase of national progress.

A central system of banks like that under the Federal Reserve Board of the United States should be created and, simultaneously, a system of industrial and agricultural banks should be brought into existence, to afford financial facilities to manufacturers, tradesmen and farmers, both large and small, throughout the country.

Complete statistics should be specially collected, giving full particulars of the material resources of the country and the employment of the people, and every facility and encouragement should be given to the public to study and discuss problems concerning their industries, occupations and material wealth, and to form a correct idea of the economic status of the country.

Coming to the more important administrative measures and changes needed, it must be premised that rapid development will be possible only when complete confidence and understanding is established between the Government and the people, that is to say, when both the central and provincial Governments become constitutional. The basic principle which should be recognized and practised is that the Government exists for the people, and that its sole business should be to place Indian interests first and to work for their advancement, at the same time helping and co-operating with the Empire.

The Indian provinces should be re-arranged and re-grouped so that, if possible, no single province may have a population of less than 10,000,000 persons. This will provide sufficient resources to enable every one of them to equip itself with the educational and other institutions that have been suggested.

The town population of India, which is very inadequate for the demands of its trade and industry, should be doubled, in order to provide the leaders, middlemen and labourers the country's work demands.

The new form of village government suggested might be introduced, so that every group of villages containing 500 to 600 dwellings, or 2,500 to 3,000 inhabitants, may have a village Government with its own officers and council, and the necessary educational and other institutions, agencies and associations for carrying on reconstruction work.

A special Reconstruction Ministry should be created both in the Central Government and in each provincial administration to recommend the appointment of commissions and committees for investigating new and important problems, to prepare new schemes of development by the study of local conditions and foreign models, to urge the provision of funds to give effect to them, to advise individual departments of Government in regard to their spheres of reconstruction work, to stimulate a spirit of initiative and self-help in the people, and to do everything needed to obtain speedy results.

A Ministry of Conservation should be created, both for the Central Government and for each province, to develop the natural resources of the country and the efficiency of the people. This commission should make an inventory of national assets in the shape of material wealth, and the intelligence and energy of the people, and at once begin to mobilize both in order to increase production and develop the people's working capacity. One of its chief functions should be to find employment for those people who have not sufficient work, and to help men of capacity and worth to find occupations for which they are most fitted, and which are congenial to them. This Ministry, like the Ministry of Reconstruction, should be only a planning and advisory authority. The executive work connected with the new measures should be done by the departments concerned, or by agencies specially created for the purpose.

A loan, beginning with Rs. 100,000,000, and rising gradually to Rs. 300,000,000 per annum, should be raised to finance education and industries. Each province should raise its own share of this loan and bear the responsibility of repayment. The loan may be repayable in thirty years, the annual charge for paying instalments of debt and interest being met from current revenues. The charge will be small at first, and within the capacity of the province to bear. It is safe to assume that, as a result of the operation of the new measures, at the end of thirty years the country will be fully able to bear the charge. Education and industry are great national functions, and education is, in a sense, a primary industry. Both these have been woefully neglected for at least a generation past, and to make up for time lost and opportunities sacrificed, they should be given a good start.

Reference has been made to the direct

action needed on the part of the people to ensure unity of purpose and ideals in their public work, and to bring into existence, independently of Government, a connected organization for the whole country for the purpose.

The ideals to be placed before the Indian public should be, politically, to change the present conditions of administration, peculiar to a dependency, to those of a self-governing Dominion like Canada; economically, to develop gradually a new system patterned upon Dominion models for production, transportation, trade, finance and banking; and socially, to raise the standard of living, and promote freer intercourse between the various communities within the country, as well as between India and foreign lands, while retaining all that is best and ennobling in the indigenous ideals and traditions. Attention should be focussed upon making India a nation economically strong, socially accomplished, and politically a self-governing unit of the British Commonwealth.

The rapid realization of these objects

depends upon securing the co-operation and support of the Government of the country, and forming an effective organization to ensure co-operative effort on the part of the people.

On a proper organization like the one suggested in the last chapter, or any parallel organization, being accepted by the majority of the nation, the people should welcome what help they can get from Government, and in directions where Government does not see eye to eye with them or cannot render help, they should have specific plans of their own as to what they are to do both for the country as a whole and in individual areas, and labour unceasingly for their realization to the best of their opportunities. Organization is the key to the situation. Nothing big can be done without organization. The point now is :—Can the nation gather up sufficient energy and make a disciplined effort in this manner by formulating and carrying into practice a comprehensive, yet simple and connected scheme of organization such as we have outlined? It would be a great victory to the forces of progress if this could be done.

A spirited propaganda should be maintained to correct the many wrong ideals in which the country abounds, and to plant new and healthy ones in their place: new ideals calculated to promote the future safety and progress of the people. Some of the methods, mottoes and precepts adopted in Western countries will be found to be suggestive. A pamphlet recently issued in a Western city, describing the city's opportunities, observed:—

> "Here is no thraldom to the past, but a trying of all things on their merits and a searching of every proposal or established institution by the one test, Will it make life happier?"

In a tramcar of another city was posted a public circular which read:—

> "You are doomed to disappointment if you sit back and expect the other man to make the city grow: there is a real job for every citizen."

Yet again, in a third city, the motto on a journal published on behalf of its business and civic interests was:—

> "Cities do not grow. They are built."

The people of every region or area should be urged not to lean on others, but to think out their problems for themselves: individual problems by self-help, and collective ones by co-ordinated effort. They should have warning that disuse of their natural powers is fatal to their progress.

When any question of importance arises, the local organization should see to it that the best minds in the locality qualified to deal with the question, study every aspect of it, take counsel together, come to sound conclusions, instruct and persuade the people and take prompt action in a collective capacity with the people's co-operation and help. It may be a question of increasing the production of a commodity, popularizing a new reform, removing an anomaly, establishing a new institution, or collecting funds for a public purpose. The rapidity with which such objects as these are accomplished will be an indication of the power of organization, of the capacity of the local community to exercise power and influence in the country by their collective effort. Knowledge is power. Capacity for co-operative effort is power. The people of any area can acquire this power, and now and then test their capacity by working out specific problems or providing for local wants as quickly as possible. One such object accomplished will put heart into the people and give them courage for further effort in the same direction.

It is not enough to keep up a few activities, to carry through a scheme here or a reform there. Things must advance all round. Every one has his bent and opportunities, and if every citizen makes a small contribution in money, time or energy, the aggregate contribution will be very considerable, and the country is bound to advance.

No right-thinking Indian who has correctly understood the comparisons instituted in an earlier chapter can escape a feeling of humiliation at the low international standing of his country. The question we have to meet is this:—Can the Indian be made to realize that his condition is capable of improvement—not for a season or two, but permanently—in ways that may give to his children opportunities of making good in the world? The task, it must be admitted, is of appalling difficulty and magnitude, but unless we believe that it is capable of accomplishment, we shall be driven to accept the pessimistic conclusion of a Western writer that India is "the dying East." That conclusion assuredly every Indian will repudiate. A consciousness should be roused in the Indian mind that a better state of things exists outside, and a vastly better state of things could be brought into existence in India itself if the people only willed and worked for the same.

INDEX

Printed by P. S. KING & SON, Ltd., Orchard House, Westminster